Walk, Run, or Retreat

The Modern School Administrator

Walk, Run, or Retreat

The Modern School Administrator

Neil V. Sullivan

with Thomas D. Wogaman and Ruth Barshay

Indiana University Press

Bloomington and London

To my wife Martha and my two sons, Roger and Michael, who understood me and were patient with me during trying times and to Ruth Barshay and Tom Wogaman for joining me in telling the story.

Acknowledgments

The authors would like to acknowledge with heartfelt thanks all of the people who helped to make this book possible. There are too many to enumerate—courageous and innovative board members, deeply concerned lay citizens, creative fellow administrators and teachers, and our office staff, Ruth Wasley, Phyllis Acton, and Isoko Umeki, who gave extra hours and extra effort cheerfully and unstintingly to type, retype, and proofread the manuscript as it was coming into being.

We want to express our special thanks to Tom's wife, Margaret, and their two young daughters, Cheryl and Diane, for their patience and generosity in giving up so many hours of family time together, so that Tom could work on the book.

We are in debt to all of these people for their encouragement and inspiration during this hectic, exciting, provocative, and satisfying period.

Contents

Walk, Run, or Retreat

The Modern School Administrator

I

Introduction

Pursuit of Relevance

Times change. Schools are changing. No one will argue the point, but why write a book about it?

Because there is a lack of understanding for the changing role of the educator, the administrator, the superintendent of schools. This lack of understanding is not restricted to the lay public, or to other staff members. Unhappily, many of my colleagues demonstrate by their words and actions that either they do not recognize the change or they fail to grasp its implications. School administrators are failing with disheartening frequency. These failures can be blamed only partially on the greater job pressures. How the superintendent meets these pressures and how he approaches his changing responsibilities account for a greater share of failures than do the pressures themselves.

Too many of my fellow superintendents are still trying to apply techniques appropriate to a generation ago. Similarly, the image of the superintendent held by teachers, students, and the general public has too frequently failed to keep up with the changing nature of his role. If the superintendent is to make his maximum impact as an educator, this confusion concerning his role must be reduced and his new role clarified.

The question remains: Why write this book? My experience in public schools includes twenty years as a superintendent of schools in widely diverse areas of this country. I have been superintendent of schools in a small rural New England community, a somewhat larger New England industrial town, an affluent Long Island suburb, and a medium-sized university city on the shores of San Francisco Bay. In addition to these public school superintendencies, I had an exciting year as superintendent of the privately supported Prince Edward County, Virginia, Free Schools project, opened for Negro children whose schools had been closed down for four years by local school authorities to avoid integration.

My length of service in education, interrupted only by World War II service in the Navy, provides another dimension to my experience. I have seen and have been part of dramatic and exciting changes in society, in schools, and in the role of the educator.

I began my career as a teacher in a one-room school in northern New Hampshire, where I earned the grand sum of eight hundred dollars a year. And, believe me, I earned every penny of it! I was the teacher, custodian, playground supervisor, bus driver, and the public relations department. The pupil-teacher ratio was forty-eight to one. That eight-hundred-dollars-a-year job was very important to me. In fact, it was the only job available to me. Why? Because Catholics in New Hampshire, and Catholics anywhere in New England, outside of Boston, had difficulty finding employment in those years. Fortunately, this situation has changed.

During those early days of my public school career, the school year lasted the traditional nine months. The school building was padlocked the day after school closed in late May or early June, and did not reopen until time to get ready for the new year in September. Today's summer school programs and other extensive summer activities reflect a change from my early rural society days and a change in the role of the school. We are now talking about year-round schools and day-and-night use of school facilities. Many American communities today are actually using their schools on an almost around-the-clock basis. Today we believe that education should never stop. High priority is given to early childhood education (children from the age of two), to adult education, and to the education of the total family. Despite this modern sophisticated thinking, there are still places in some of our fifty states where the kindergarten program is not available and where adult classes not only are not held, but have not even been considered.

In my early days as an educator, the curriculum was oriented around the three Rs. Today we are including family living, sex education, black history, Swahili, foreign language in grade four, mathematics, linguistics, English as a second language, and a host of other topics either ignored, tabooed, or unknown in the old days. In addition, we are now teaching in our secondary schools most of the subjects that twenty years ago were taught only to college freshmen and sophomores.

In those early days the parents assumed responsibility for feeding the child. Today the school cafeteria is big business.

Many years ago rural America was dotted with small one- or two-room schools within what was then considered reasonable walking distance for youngsters. Since then there has been a sweeping trend toward closing these schools, consolidating them into the towns, and transporting the children to and from school in buses. Today almost twenty million boys and girls in rural, urban, and suburban America ride buses to and from school. Today we are moving toward closing neighborhood schools that range from a capacity of three hundred children to one thousand children. We are talking about educational parks, and this talking in some communities has resulted in action. We are talking about five large high schools in a large city to replace twenty-five medium sized high schools. We are talking about a school-within-a-school concept with several thousand students coming together on a single campus.

During my first years as a superintendent I was the decision maker. I decided what books to buy, what subjects to teach, and when to teach them. I also recommended the salaries for teachers and decided whether or not a teacher would be asked to return to the school district for another school year. I was not bound by tenure laws nor did I have to negotiate salaries with labor unions or militant groups representing the establishment. All of this has changed. Today these subjects are handled either through collective bargaining or by negotiating councils. Today the decision-making power is shared by many. The classroom teacher has a greatly expanded role in decision making; so do interested members of the lay public. The autocratic, paternalistic superintendent is moribund, if not already dead.

In those early days as a superintendent I was a little like the local minister. I was considered the absolute authority in my field, but was expected to maintain silence on any subject other than local education. I was to hear no evil, speak no evil, see no evil. Today's superintendent is no longer regarded as the absolute authority in his own field or any other, but he does have greater freedom to exercise influence on other issues affecting society. However, few of my colleagues take advantage of this new freedom. It is rare for a public school administrator to speak out on controversial issues, even those that affect the very lives of the students he is trying to teach. Major issues such as the war in Vietnam, policy brutality, the Negro crisis, civil rights, the population explosion, are generally met with silence by the average school superintendent. Great political battles are fought for important positions such as the Presidency of the United States, a seat in the United States Senate, or the governorship of a state. Here again, the school administrator has abstained. Abstention, vacillation, and procrastination are the mode for the typical American schoolman.

Again, why do I write this book? Because I would like to share my experiences and the insight I have gained from them. Many school administrators will see in some of my experiences similarities to their own. I shall try to avoid technical educational jargon because it is sometimes meaningless to people outside the profession; and, too, it is often used to impress or confuse, rather than to describe precisely or explain. Hopefully, my colleagues, and lay citizens who are interested in the directions our society and our schools are taking, will find my book stimulating and valuable.

I hope the experiences I share with you on these pages will encourage school superintendents and boards of education to take a bold new look at their conduct and their performance, and to take new directions to meet the intricate and challenging problems of today's youth. Hopefully, an increasing number of school superintendents will be encouraged to take positive steps in implementing programs designed for the 1970s and 1980s and to move away from the programs that met some of the needs of some of the children in the 1920s and 1930s, but are no longer useful in the space age.

From these experiences may come school superintendents who place a higher priority on the characteristic of adaptability and a lower priority on rigidity, a higher priority on boldness and a lower priority on timidity, a higher priority on equal educational opportunities for all children and a lower priority on meeting the needs of the affluent, a higher priority on involving students and parents in decision making and a lower priority on autocratic decision making by the privileged few.

2

School District Politics

Beware the Pitfalls

For the past twenty years I have served as a public school superintendent. I have been one of the approximately sixteen thousand and have served in four different states. I have come to know many superintendents intimately, and, by and large, to understand them. They are predominantly—almost exclusively —white Anglo-Saxons, male, fiftyish, former high school teachers, then high school principals. A high percentage have been coaches of athletic teams where they were given local exposure in the press.

The men are almost always married (generally to a teacher), have two or three children, and have served in one of the wars. Once back in civilian life they have joined the American Legion and usually the local Rotary Club. On Sunday mornings, almost without exception, they attend church with their families.

They vote on election day, but play it close to the vest trying not to reveal the candidate of their choice or the political party to which they belong. They generally are members of the "in party." On controversial issues they remain silent. They usually take no public positions on subjects such as Vietnam, the draft, or birth control.

They are great convention goers, never missing an opportunity to attend the American Association of School Administrators meeting in Atlantic City, the state meetings, or the regional meetings which are usually held in tourist fun areas. Like most middle-aged men, they like their liquor. They are very careful on the home front about where they buy their liquor and with whom they share it, but once away from their home town they usually live it up.

On the firing line they have run a tight ship—at least they did until the recent explosions in some of our city school systems. They maintained a status quo school organization based on the Armed Service chain-of-command operation. Teachers would funnel their concerns to them through department heads, to the principal, and on up the administration ladder. The reply would go back down the same way. If it was a direct reply to the teacher, all hands—but *all* hands—would receive copies. In general, individual teachers have not been encouraged to come to headquarters with their suggestions.

Local superintendents have an enviable record for great integrity, while scandals involving other municipal departments make headlines in the nation's press. I cannot recall a single incident of a school superintendent straying from the straight and honest role. School superintendents, collectively, have handled billions of dollars, and have watched over every penny of it as they would their own money. They have been reliable guardians of public funds and have distinguished themselves by their scrupulous handling of these funds.

They have also zealously guarded a school system (that they helped structure) designed for middle-class children. As a group, over the years, they have not looked favorably on change and agents of change. In their defense it must be said that they rarely had budgets that made much experimentation possible and were almost penniless when it came to financial support for research. Also, in their defense, most of their school systems structured for white Anglo-Saxons did the job in acceptable fashion because their schools served predominantly middle-class children. Superintendents were asked to prepare students to pass college board exams, and this became the only and ultimate goal in many school systems. They staffed their schools with middle-class Anglo-Saxons trained in institutions of higher education to aim at that goal—and aim they did.

Once an educator became superintendent of schools, he rarely went back to the scene of the action—the classroom. He became bogged down with the minutiae of the assignment, worked full days, long evenings, and full weeks meeting parents who lined up with their complaints, attending PTA meetings, hearing the ladies decide such great questions as what refreshments to have at their next PTA meeting, spending considerable time with textbook salesmen and vendors peddling everything from sweet-smelling material for the boys' urinals to furniture, and always making himself available to school board members no matter when they called. As superintendent he could seldom find time to get into the schools. His intentions probably were good, but the fact of the matter is that school superintendents seldom visit classrooms. As a result, a dichotomy has developed in a great many of our school systems between the teacher and the central administration.

The schism between administrators and teachers started when administrators decided that generally they represented the board of education and simply could not find time to meet, visit, or relate personally to the teachers and to teacher organizations. The teachers responded to this situation by saying, "You have no time for us; you don't understand our problems; you don't really represent us." The dichotomy between teachers and superintendents was finally made official by the American Federation of Teachers when they restricted their membership to exclude school administrators.

School superintendents too often find themselves figuratively married to boards of education and alienated from teachers and teacher organizations. As they move up from the teachers' circle to the board circle, they find a marked difference in the composition of the two groups. The teachers include in their circle lower middle-class, young and old, moderate to liberal individuals, most of whom are struggling economically to make a go of it. The breadwinner is generally the male, and often he is enrolled in a graduate school program attempting to earn an advanced degree in his major field. His salary is in the low to medium range, but his expenses are above that range. He finds himself unable to put any money aside for savings. He is constantly pushing for high salaries and unfortunately sees his superintendent and the board of education as adversaries.

The superintendent, on the other hand, has moved up to a higher social and economic circle. He finds that he is accepted by his board of education friends, the doctor, the lawyer, and the realtor. He goes to their parties, listens to their dialogue, and ends up being one of them in the eyes of his teachers.

The dichotomy deepens as the teachers militantly band together, trusting only members of their own organization, and the superintendent joins forces with the power structure in the community. The teachers now find it necessary to employ counsel to represent their point of view at salary negotiation time, and the superintendent finds himself on the side of the board of education. In this unfortunate labor-management situation, the superintendent has aligned himself with management.

The net result is that the teachers turn to their own group for leadership and the superintendent can no longer represent his professional colleagues in a discussion of critical views affecting public education. The split usually starts over salary negotiations but goes on to cover the gamut of school activities. Suddenly the superintendent finds that his opinions are not welcome in areas of curriculum, program, and personnel. He has been cut off from the masses, from his former colleagues, and now he joins the middle-class, formal organization in the struggle to control public education.

His troubles are just beginning. Board members need broad popular support to be reelected and cannot alienate any segment of the community in their campaign for voter support. It is not unusual, therefore, for them to court teacher organizations on Saturday and the Chamber of Commerce on Sunday. Deals are often made and the superintendent finds himself caught in the conflict without any formal support. Many times he ends up on the outside looking in. He may be dismissed or he may be permitted to serve out the last few years of his contract. He is confused about his future and trusts no one.

Now we find a man grasping for straws. He is too old to go back to the classroom or to be wanted by another school system. So he tries desperately to please his employer, the board of education, and in his anxiety becomes ineffectual as a leader of the professional staff. The result is a divided school system struggling, without a leader, for survival and for the support of the community—a school system unable to meet the needs of the students or the staff.

What do superintendents talk about at their innumerable conferences and conventions? Do they spend their spare time reviewing pertinent features of new programs? Some do, of course, but more often they discuss ways and means of retiring early. They refer to "unmanageable situations" and express a desire to "get away from it all." They blame the new union, the aggressiveness of minority groups, and the recalcitrant taxpayers, but they rarely accept even partial responsibility for the situation. Or they talk about the program they know best: the interscholastic athletic program. They know, after all, that their administration is frequently judged by the win and loss record of the local high school's football team.

School administrators, particularly in small and middle-sized communities, rarely make a move until they know which way the wind is blowing. They determine the direction, the supposed mood of the community, by keeping their ears close to the establishment: by attending weekly Rotary Club meetings and tuning in on how the doctors feel about local problems, how the bankers feel about a tax increase, what the realtors are saying about where the next neighborhood school should be built, and how the clergy feel about rock concerts. Of course, after they carefully tune in on all of these fronts, they hold back until they check out their findings with a "majority of the Board of Education."

School superintendents are fully aware of the two organizations in the community—the formal and the informal. They know that the formal organization usually waits until matters have been cleared with the real power people, that informal organization made up of a few bankers, a few industrialists, one of the doctors who has made a million or two, and probably the local judge. This informal group differs somewhat from city to city, but it does exist in every community and must be reckoned with.

Although the conditions are different in our larger cities, many of the same dimensions are there—formal and informal power structures, teacher organizations that do not trust the administration, administrators who stay close to the establishment and fear the teacher organizations, and a curriculum that is designed for middle-class children despite the fact that the larger number of children attending the public schools are minority group children.

Conditions in our large city schools did not change drastically until chaos occurred in many of them. Until then, city superintendents and boards of education refused to believe that the militant minorities had the power to affect change. The Supreme Court decision, *Brown* v. *Board of Education*, was largely ignored and districts went merrily on, building in segregation by constructing one small neighborhood school after another, employing middle-class Oriental and white teachers, and supporting a curriculum that ignored contributions of the minorities and was totally irrelevant to the interests of minority students. Not until black student unions were organized, made demands, and closed many schools, did city school superintendents and boards of education become responsive to the needs of all students.

Most school superintendents in small, medium, and large cities have been cut from the same cloth and have reacted in the same way. Most large city superintendents cut their teeth in small communities and did not change their philosophy when they moved up to the larger community. They reluctantly—in the mid-sixties—involved organizations such as NAACP, CORE, and the Urban League in deliberations. Not until black men and women started to appear on boards of education in ever-increasing numbers did some of the boards begin to respond to the needs of minority students. Why were they so slow to respond? Because white middle-class Americans continued through the mid-sixties to hold a majority of seats on city councils and boards of education, and the boards of education determined the superintendents' salaries and tenures of office. The superintendents held out—and continue to hold out in our cities —as long as minority groups did not seize a majority of seats on the boards of education.

Political parties have had a major influence on how large city school systems operate, but have had little influence on the medium and small communities. Until a few years ago, political opportunists used membership on the board of education as a stepping stone to a higher political position. They literally *used* the school to build an organization around patronage. Teachers were employed after it was clear to all concerned that Mr. X said a good word, school sites were approved when a friendly nod was given, and innumerable contracts, ranging from the fuel needed to heat the school plants to the paper and pencils used by the children, all were properly approved by the board. Generally, the action was aboveboard and no overt pressure or influence was used by the board member. A position on the board of education, however, before 1960, provided an aspiring politician with many opportunities to perform little favors for people, thus building support for his candidacy in future elections.

All of this changed in the cities, when tough, gutty questions had to be resolved at public meetings of the school board. The assignment no longer permitted an individual to build small empires. Instead, the board member found himself caught in some difficult and controversial public issues. Teachers became increasingly militant, and strikes were not unusual. Students walked out on the slightest provocation and closed schools down in one city after another. Anti-war demonstrations started on school campuses. "Mothers for Neighborhood Schools" demonstrated. Anti-busing groups sprang up in every community. The local property tax suddenly reached the saturation point. Almost overnight a place on a city board of education became a burying ground for aspiring politicians.

But through all of this the public school superintendents have, by and large, hung on—many by the skin of their teeth. Others, particularly in the larger communities, have retired, and some have just plain been fired.

The great school systems, almost without exception, are built by strong boards of education who have the intelligence and courage to select an outstanding educator as their superintendent. They then develop policy that is fair to all concerned, and turn the daily operation of the schools over to the superintendent.

The superintendent in turn must select a staff that has demonstrated ability, must set the tone for all by working diligently with them on critical issues, and must demonstrate courage by refusing to be coerced by school board, fellow staff members, students, or parents. He must accept constructive suggestions graciously and give credit to those making the suggestions. He must discipline privately those who need disciplining. He must acknowledge that he is only one member of a much larger team and must encourage the entire staff to try new creative approaches. He must avoid hasty decisions when time permits study, but have the courage to make an on-the-spot decision when conditions seem to warrant action and delay would be vacillation. He must establish the ground rules *with* staff, school board, parents, and students—not *for* them. He must keep his cool when under attack and surround himself with individuals who have the ability to fill his shoes at any time. He must join in setting realistic goals and objectives, and then leave no stone unturned to see that these goals are attained. And above all, he must keep the channels of communication wide open at every level of the school system.

3

The Superintendent and His Family

From the Inside Looking Out

The city was where it all started for me—Manchester, a textile city in southern New Hampshire. My father was an immigrant and, at the time of my birth, a bartender in one of Manchester's hotels. Three years later, with the passage of the Volstead Act in 1918, he was the unemployed father of four young children and things went from bad to worse. Jobs grew scarce when the textile mills closed in the mid-twenties and never reopened.

The depression came early to Manchester and the family was trapped. As I recall, my father was unable to earn more than $25 a week as a laborer and my mother became one of the great managers of all time. She had one driving ambition—to educate her children. She tried with a great vengeance. When the Catholic Church announced that all Catholic children must attend parochial school, she complied until it was obvious to her that although we were learning our prayers we were not being educated. She decided to teach us the prayers, somehow made peace with the church, and maneuvered the four children into predominantly middle-class schools.

We lived on the fringe of the Irish ghetto and could have gone either direction. She made the big decision: go to the middle-class school. I learned much from the experience—that my clothes were different, but, in general, cleaner than those of my classmates—that my language was different and at times provoked laughter from my classmates—that I had trouble with *was* and *were*, *can* and *may*, *these* and *those*. But I managed to survive without too many problems. I could do some things better than they could (arithmetic), and they constantly challenged me to improve in the other subjects. For example, the teachers in reading would permit you to read until you made a mistake. I read with a passion and learned to attack new words with conviction because I wanted to stand up as long as they did.

When it was time to go to high school, all my affluent classmates selected the college course. That is where they were expected to go and that is what they planned to do. So I made my plans exactly the same way. I signed up for English, biology, French, algebra, and history. I avoided the vocational subjects— general science and general math.

Four years later I was prepared to go to college, but with a father working three days a week I could not set my goal too high. I worked with my brothers during the summer peddling vegetables, saved $150 each summer, and entered the State Normal School in Keene, where I remained for three years. I participated in everything because I knew that job placement depended on having a school record that included a well-rounded list of activities. I was in the Forensic Society, took part in dramatics, was captain of the college basketball team and president of my class. I graduated (in three years) in 1936, and as I sought employment in New Hampshire I suddenly realized that to be a Catholic was unfortunate—unfortunate, that is, if you were seeking employment as a teacher outside the city of Manchester. The president of the class of 1936 was the last member of the class to be employed. I was happy to take that little old one-room school in Glencliff for an annual salary of $800.

My wife, Martha, knew the name of the game, too. She started teaching one year after I did, in the late thirties, in a two-room school for $850 a year. We were married in 1941 when I finished work on my Master's degree at Columbia University, and we went to live in Newport, New Hampshire, where I had my first secondary school assignment—teaching mathematics and science at a salary of $1,500. Just imagine—almost doubling your salary in five years! I was in seventh heaven.

Our first son, Roger, was born the following July in Portsmouth, where I had taken a job that summer. I was employed as a laborer at $54 a week. This was $15 a week more than I was making during the year as a school teacher, but I earned every last cent of it. I was given a pair of rubber boots, a hard hat, and a shovel, then I descended a few hundred feet below sea level and shoveled mud into huge buckets. Hard work, but it paid the hospital bills. I saved enough that summer to move the family to Biddeford, Maine, where I taught math and science and coached football, baseball, and basketball for $1,800 a year.

In order to make both ends meet, Martha made her own clothes (and the baby's), planted a garden and canned the vegetables we raised, did a little substitute teaching, and spent her evenings waiting for me to come home from one school event or another. I carried a sandwich for lunch, and night after night I was involved with the students. Fortunately, another young couple was also involved in the same way. Dave would remain with me at school and Anne would spend the evenings with Martha. I had been out of school since 1936; I had a lovely, devoted wife and a young son—what more could a fellow ask!

But by then our country had been plunged into World War II. I enlisted in the Navy midway through the year, and the Navy saw to it that I had time to think about my profession. I had plenty of time to think—first, on a destroyer escort in the North Atlantic, then on a destroyer doing anti-submarine work in the same ocean. When the war in Europe was over, I went to Guam, Iwo, and Okinawa in the Pacific theater of operations. Yes, I had lots of time to think.

When I left the Navy I went right back to my profession. But now I had one goal in mind: I wanted to be the top guy, the superintendent—to make the decisions—to be free to be my own man. As things turned out, I was to become a superintendent much sooner than I had planned.

In 1948, at the age of thirty-three, I became the youngest school superintendent in Maine at that time. I was serving as a high school principal in Jay, Maine, when the incumbent superintendent (who had been on the job only three months) resigned for personal reasons. He had succeeded an old-timer who had served as the district superintendent for as long as most of the natives could remember. The old fellow not only ran the schools, but he also owned, managed, and operated the coal, wood, and ice business in the village of Wilton.

My starting salary was $3,600, subject to the approval of the local people at their annual town meeting held on the first Monday in March, weather permitting. My salary was divided between the two towns in the district, Jay and Wilton, each raising $1,800. I'll never forget that first meeting and the first motion made: "I move that for the next full year we set the superintendent's salary at $900." That really shook me up. That was a 50 percent cut and I could not afford that. Furthermore, I didn't like the principle of the thing—where would this stop! Well, fortunately the motion never got off the ground for lack of a second.

But things did not change much for the Sullivans. We had another son, Michael, born in 1945. Instead of $1,500 annually I was making $3,600, but there were four of us now instead of two. Martha compensated by planting a bigger garden and staying up later at night to make more clothes. Did I have more time at home? Hardly! Board meetings, faculty meetings, and speaking before any group willing to listen, kept me out almost every night.

I mention this experience because school people, like most lower income groups, are constantly fighting for economic survival—and this has a deleterious effect on the profession. A young administrator is never sure what will happen to his salary or his job, so he does what the local school board desires. He behaves properly at all times, his language is always impeccable, and he and his family are always well-groomed. This is particularly true in small towns. The community expects him to behave and live in a fashion similar to that of the local minister and his family.

His salary permits no luxuries and limits his social mobility. No money to join the Country Club for a round of golf. No extended family trips to other parts of the country or to other countries. No money for investment. Perhaps a few dollars to join a book club. He doesn't have enough loose change to do anything but exist. Most schoolmen work a lifetime in the profession, and—like most lower income people—have nothing at retirement but what the state provides them in the form of a bare bones retirement program.

The wife and children of the schoolman had better be endowed with all the graces God bestows upon wives and children in order that they might survive. My wife and children were so blessed. Roger was five the year I became school superintendent, and he was going to have to go to a one-room school. (I was knocking myself out trying to close them without too much success.) Martha attended one of those delightful neighborhood meetings and stated quite categorically that she would keep Roger home rather than send him to the one-room school. Well, now, Mrs. Wife of the Superintendent, how dare you! Wives of superintendents are supposed to be seen, not heard!

Martha used beautiful judgment about her relations with the boys' teachers. She kept away from them, came when other parents came, approached them only when a real question about the boys' schoolwork occurred, but let it be known that she was always available if the teacher wanted to communicate with her.

I, in turn, made it clear that I was deeply interested in my sons' progress, but also kept away from their teachers.

But it wasn't easy. I recall one meeting in Sanford when an irate father charged me with using my influence as superintendent to make the football coach unfairly play my son Roger in a football game the Saturday before. Roger just happened to be a talented athlete (he won top awards in four sports and was recruited by most of the major universities in the country) and the coach was undoubtedly one of the most ethical men who ever coached a group of boys. But that night that father not only was mad at the coach, he was furious with the whole Sullivan family —and told me so.

Because Roger was the son of the superintendent, some of his coaches and teachers expected more of him than of any of the other boys. They expected a decorum that was a tremendous challenge for any adolescent. I must say that he reacted well to the challenge and seemed to thrive on the pressures. Michael generally stayed on top of things, too. What problems he had were not of an academic nature. He was a sensitive youngster with a strong social consciousness and sense of justice. He would pop off in class and take positions that were not always popular with some of his teachers. He also lived in the shadow of his older brother and twice as much was expected of him. But he survived beautifully, graduated from the Berkeley campus of the University of California, and now is in Graduate School in the Boston area. Neither son ever complained about his treatment by teachers, and both were privileged to attend some of the best schools in our country and to have some of the nation's finest teachers.

We also learned early in the game that a superintendent of schools had to select his friends carefully—at least that's what he was expected to do. I was convinced that it would damage staff morale if Martha and I made close friends of any of the immediate school staff, teachers, or administrators. We followed that practice and it wasn't easy. We had some of the finest people in the world on our faculties, but we did not develop a close relationship with any of them. I rationalized my position on the basis of fairness. I could not entertain all of them, so I would not entertain any of them. Also, I disliked becoming so involved with school personnel outside of school that my judgment might be influenced if I had to make a decision regarding a contract or a raise or any other question of a professional nature. This policy resulted in my getting to know other people and their getting to know Martha and me and our boys. We often limited our close friends to one family, but in our home we entertained people of all walks of life—the parents of our boys' playmates, the Catholic priest, a minister and his wife, a few doctors, city council members, the Mayor, always a few of the black community, the girls from the office, university chancellors, congressmen, and lots and lots of everyday people. (The one year I scrapped the "Sullivan Plan" was in Prince Edward County. In that situation the school family was just one, big, happy family. See *Bound for Freedom.*)

I took a very active part in community affairs—particularly youth activities. I served as commissioner of the Little League, chairman of Red Cross drives, Red Feather Chairman, and I met with young people and their parents at every opportunity. I enjoyed every minute of it, and so did Martha. She had her own Cub Scout group, tutored any child in the neighborhood in need of tutoring, and would lend a helping hand at PTA dinners or any fund raising activity where she could help.

Martha also found her interests in her home. She loved doing things for me and for the boys. She accepted my idiosyncrasies and stood up well when I was attacked. She learned to let me make all the decisions on the schools, although if I asked her for an opinion she gave it willingly. But there was never any pressure from her, no second guessing. She was always there when

I needed her. She got along splendidly with other women, and all the young people who came to the house fell in love with Martha. But best of all, she is a great mother and this is mighty important if your children are to thrive. I was out so much—particularly in the evening—that if Martha had not been willing to sacrifice herself (although she never felt that she was "sacrificing"), my two sons would have been brought up by baby sitters. Martha was, and is, a great hostess. She loves to cook and can make the best apple pie and lemon pie to be found anywhere. She thoroughly enjoyed preparing food for our friends and decorating and redecorating our home. I am very fortunate to be blessed with such a remarkable wife.

I got my extracurricular kicks out of keeping young with my boys and their buddies. We skied together from the time they were three and five, went hunting together, and would go to the gym and play basketball. But the most fun of all was when the family went off each summer on great camping trips. We pitched our tent in forty-seven of the fifty states (missed Rhode Island, Alaska, and Hawaii) and every province in Canada and Mexico. We spent endless hours planning the trips during the winter and then had the time of our lives camping together, swimming, hiking, building the camp fires, visiting city museums and state capitals, doing our own cooking—and I could forget school buses, one-room schools, closed mills, and new vocational schools.

When the boys went off to college, I joined the Y. I went daily (still do), would run a few miles, row, ride a bike, and take a steam bath. I met great people at the Y. They knew who I was but kept off the subject of school integration, grouping, and teaching. Instead, we talked about physical fitness and sports and people—not school talk.

I have mentioned these things because they are important. My family lived through those early difficult years and grew strong from the experience. But I hope that our society will come to reward our teachers and administrators in a manner that will make them as independent as other people—not rich over night, but able to save a few dollars before retirement, to have enough money to send the kids to camp, to buy a few things extra for your wife—and yes, maybe make it possible for Papa to join the Country Club before he is sixty.

But even more important, structure the job so that our educators and their families can be free—free to speak out—free to dress the way they wish—free to support openly the candidates of their choice—free to choose their friends——free to enjoy a very challenging and rewarding life in the profession of education.

4

The Superintendent and His Staff

The Descent From Olympus

Any discussion of the relationship between the modern super-intendent and his staff should start by pronouncing a benediction on paternalism. The superintendent is no longer seen as the "Great White Father," nor as the source of infallible wisdom. This figurative descent from Olympus has been hastened by two developments: the increasing complexity of public education (the days are gone when one man can literally "know it all"), and the attraction to the profession of an increasing number of teachers and other staff members who do not need a father figure (and who, in fact, will not accept one in their professional lives).

The man who needs the kind of adulation formerly associated with the position of superintendent had better find some other field—for his own sake and for the sake of public education. He will find himself constantly frustrated by the refusal of his staff to consider him an oracle, and his efforts to reign as "Big Chief" will get in the way of his genuine leadership. Respect for his leadership must be based on something more than a "divine right" respect for the office he holds. Only mutual respect between the superintendent and his staff—teachers and non-teachers—can create an effective working relationship aimed toward excellence in education for all.

In the present era, public education, except in the very small-
est districts, has become far too complex a business to be adequately administered by one man. The recent tendency toward
consolidation throughout the country has reduced the number
of districts and has made the districts larger. The typical superintendent finds himself responsible for a school district with a
greater number of students, teachers, and school buildings. The
district is also larger in terms of geography, and the population
being served is typically larger and more diverse than ever
before. The needs of students also have become more complex,
making more demands of the schools, the administrators, and
the teachers. The responsibilities undertaken by the schools have
increased to meet the expectations of the public. All of this leads
to the inescapable conclusion that the era of the "one strong
man" type of superintendent is over. No one person, by himself,
can adequately fulfill demands made upon the superintendency.

As the "iron man" superintendent disappears, the concept of
the superintendency team rises, particularly in medium and
larger districts. Under this concept the superintendent gathers
around him a team of colleagues who collectively provide the
administrative leadership for the district. Each member of this
team carries an individual area of responsibility. Each one has
part of the load that formerly was the responsibility of the superintendent alone. The team members pool their talents, ideas, and
personal resources to lend general leadership to the district.
Under this arrangement the superintendent retains the ultimate
responsibility for the success or the failure of the administration,
but he is relieved from having to perform personally all of the
tasks associated with his district's administration. Furthermore,
he is relieved of having to maintain the pretense that he knows
equally well every facet of school administration. He can freely
concede that there are areas in which subordinates have far
better knowledge of details than he does.

Far from detracting from the personal power of the superintendent, the team concept increases the superintendent's impact. His influence is felt, through the actions of his team members, in far wider circles than he could hope to reach by acting alone.

Because of the crucial role of the superintendency team in administering and leading the school district, the development and utilization of the team must be carefully scrutinized and nurtured. The specific makeup of this team will vary from district to district and from superintendent to superintendent, but certain basic principles are essential.

It should be axiomatic that the superintendent have a free hand in selecting the members of this team and in developing their assignments. The superintendency team is an extension of the superintendent himself. If he is to be held accountable for the team's operation, he must have the freedom to use his judgment in selecting and deploying team members.

Members of the team should reflect a variety of skills and areas of expertise. This is no place for rubber stamps of the superintendent himself. Rather, the superintendent should surround himself with individuals who can assume responsibility for specialized fields and who can complement the superintendent and the other members of the team in the background each brings to his job.

Each member of the team must be personally and professionally loyal to the superintendent. This, again, should be obvious, but it is so important that it needs to be stressed. Each member of the team must believe in the philosophy of the administration and in its goals. Each person must have confidence in the superintendent as a leader in the attainment of these goals. The team members must also be loyal to each other. There can and should and will be differing views concerning possible courses of action, and undoubtedly disagreements will arise. But loyalty to the team and respect for its purposes should leave no room or time for personal rancor. Each team member should be geared to helping the team as a whole to be successful. The superintendent owes the same loyalty to the members of his team as he expects from them, and as he expects them to have for each other.

The areas of responsibility must be sufficiently well-defined so that each team member knows what is expected of him. In the best of organizations there are examples of undue overlap as well as instances in which specific problems fall between the separate responsibilities of team members. It is the superintendent's responsibility to see that overlapping is kept to a minimum and that no problem is overlooked because no team member assumed responsibility for it.

Once members of the team know their responsibilities, they should be free to fulfill them. The superintendent must have sufficient confidence in his associates to permit them to work on problems without constantly looking over their shoulders. This is not always easy to do, but it must be done if the team is to develop the degree of initiative necessary to share the load. The superintendent, of course, must insist upon results, and must keep informed as his associates proceed with their responsibilities.

Ground rules need to be established for the functioning of the team. These ground rules must include open channels of communication with each other and with the superintendent. These channels will include meetings, either regularly scheduled or specially arranged, as well as individual contacts as various situations may require.

Members of the team should be picked not only on the basis of their individual skills and areas of expertise but also on their general ability to relate to people and to analyze logically problems of a general nature. The superintendent's team members frequently will be representing him to the public or with other relevant individuals and groups. They must, therefore, be able to get along well with people and to present a positive image of the administration as a whole.

During my Berkeley administration, I was fortunate in being able to develop an administrative team that can serve as a prototype to illustrate the points made above. When I went to Berkeley I found that most of the top members of the preceding administration had either retired or moved to other communities, thus creating a break in the continuity of organization. But it had the beneficial effect of giving me virtually a free hand in selecting the people to work with me and form my team.

I was named for the position in early spring of 1964, but could not take over formally until September first, because of commitments in Prince Edward County. During the intervening period I visited Berkeley about once a month for two or three days at a time. This gave me the chance to become acquainted with possible leaders, to become familiar with the problems of the district, and to put together my own team. Although I recruited three or four principals and one director from outside the organization, most of the people named to top positions were already staff members of the Berkeley schools. The important thing, however, is that I was able to select them personally and, before their appointment, to become satisfied that we could work effectively together.

During the first few months I replaced the cabinet meetings of the previous regime with relatively informal weekly meetings for various combinations of top administrators. By the end of the first year, however, we had developed a structure that was to serve as my central administrative team for the balance of my administration in Berkeley. We named it the "Superintendent's Administrative Council." The group came to be known as SAC throughout the district and community. SAC functioned as the kind of superintendency team I have been talking about.

SAC's membership included the superintendent, the assistant superintendent for instruction, my administrative assistant (one of the co-authors of this book), and the directors of business services, personnel, elementary education, secondary education, and special education. During my final year in Berkeley the office of human relations was given director status and its director also became a member of SAC.

The members of SAC, both individually and collectively, were one of the most competent groups of people with whom I have had the privilege of working. Each individual brought a unique background and set of skills. Each was a real pro in his respective area of responsibility. But it was considerably more than a collection of people who could adequately administer their separate departments. This group collectively acquired great skill in brain-storming general problems facing the district, as well as in providing help with issues or questions centering in the area of any one of the members.

Tuesday mornings at nine thirty were established as SAC's regular meeting time. The meetings varied in length. Some lasted an hour or two. Other meetings would continue for an entire day. My administrative assistant maintained both the agenda and the minutes. Any member had the prerogative of submitting items for the agenda in advance. We were sufficiently flexible, however, that late items could be brought up. The meetings were frequently joined by individual staff members who carried responsibilities relating to topics under discussion.

SAC meetings were the frequent scenes of general brain-storming and wrestling with strategic problems facing the district. Topics ranged from the relatively minor to some of the most fundamental issues that could face an American school system. The group many times demonstrated its value both as a deliberative—albeit advisory—body to think through possible solutions to problems and as a team in implementing those solutions once they had been decided upon.

Most of the discussion so far has centered around the superintendent's own team. This is a *sine qua non* for a successful school administration. However, the staff concerns of the modern superintendent extend far beyond this limited circle. If school districts are to fulfill demands placed upon them, they must have the best personnel available—the best teachers, the best specialists, the best middle management. Without top-caliber people in all parts of the staff, the impact of even the most enlightened and most effective central administration will be reduced.

The competition for top-flight people at all levels is severe. It takes far more to attract and hold the kind of people we are talking about than a good salary schedule, good fringe benefits, and good working conditions. The people I am talking about look beyond these things and examine the general climate— what the district is trying to accomplish, the attitudes of the district toward students and toward education, the chances for personal and professional success, and the chances for making a real contribution. A district that is on the move and can communicate that fact is at a decided advantage in attracting people to whom the public schools are considerably more than simply a means of earning a livelihood. Of course, the new breed of school staff member insists upon salary and other employment conditions that are in keeping with the importance of his role, but he is equally concerned that his professional life count for something. Thus, districts that want to "come alive" must emphasize the challenge as well as the benefits of working there.

After top people have been employed, they must be utilized so that their creativity is encouraged and their talents can obtain maximum results. To employ vital, imaginative, creative staff members and then attempt to force them into a mold or stifle their creativity is a waste and a danger. The kind of educators

I am talking about will not tolerate such stifling. They will accept the necessary organization and will respect strong leadership, but the organization and the leadership must be perceived as aids in accomplishing the task, rather than as unnecessary restraints.

In addition to acquiring a top-flight staff, the superintendent must develop effective means of communicating with that staff if he is to be a successful leader. Breakdowns at this point are among the most common causes of administrative failure. The rising militancy among teachers makes it doubly important that lines of communication be clear. There are enough points over which staff members will honestly disagree with each other in principle; we cannot afford the luxury of disagreements caused through misunderstanding or failure to communicate with each other.

Communication, of course, operates at several levels. At the simplest level, staff members need to be informed. This can be accomplished largely through memos or announcements to groups. On a higher level, however, there is a need not only for information but for an understanding of where we are going, what we are trying to accomplish, some of the problems we are facing, etc. Communication must go beyond the mere exchange of information and concern itself with the development of mutual trust and of respect for each other's ideas.

In Berkeley we developed many techniques. The morning following each regular school board meeting, a mimeographed resumé of that meeting entitled "The Morning After" was sent to the entire staff. Throughout my tenure there, I met monthly with a Superintendent's Teachers Advisory Council (STAC), which consisted of one or more teachers *elected by the faculty* from each school. Most of the discussions consisted of items dealing with one or more local situations, but STAC's presence served as a means of coming to grips with much larger issues as they arose in the district. It was also a useful means of keeping abreast of the concerns being felt in various local schools. Various members of my staff and I also met with local school faculties, sometimes combining two or more school faculties in one session. We also held frequent breakfast sessions with the leaders of both teacher organizations.

Other techniques were utilized from time to time. It is up to the superintendent to develop techniques that work within his own district. Whatever the methods used, the lines of communication must be understood, be clear, and be two way. The superintendent needs to receive the input from his staff as well as to keep his staff informed concerning his own plans. Communication lines should stimulate interaction on a multi-dimensional level among the staff members. If the lines of communication are effective and unobstructed, district staff can function as a team.

The role of the educator and his relationship to his staff have undergone sweeping changes. No longer is the "divine right" of administrators recognized as sufficient reason to respect a superintendent's leadership. Gone is the era in which one man can effectively administer a district by depending upon his own resources. He needs a team of individuals who are competent in different areas of school administration, who can work together effectively in attacking general problems facing the district, and who are both personally and professionally loyal to the administration. The modern superintendent must actively seek and then properly utilize competent and creative personnel at all levels of the district's organization. He must further develop effective two-way communication with that staff and seek actively to develop trust and respect between himself and staff members. The manner in which the superintendent develops and utilizes the staff will determine whether or not the district will be successful under his leadership.

5

The Superintendent and the Teacher

Management and Labor?

Teachers: they come in all shapes and sizes, all races and religions, both male and female, and range in age from their late teens to the seventies and eighties, depending on state and local limitation.

Teachers: they represent the spectrum of political philosophies ranging from the far right reactionary to the far left political activist, from Deweyite to traditionalist, from Republican to Democrat, from supporters of Eugene McCarthy to supporters of Governor Wallace, and all shades in between.

Teachers: they are Catholic and Protestant, Jew and Gentile, Mormon, Quaker, Baptist, Methodist, Presbyterian, and Congregationalist; atheist and agnostic and Unitarian Universalist; Mohammedan and Buddhist.

Teachers: they are narrow-minded and broad-minded; they have positive attitudes and negative attitudes; some are interested in the sciences, some in the humanities. Some enjoy the great outdoors, while others cannot tolerate nature or those who enjoy it. Some read the great novels, others read nothing but the sports pages of the local newspaper.

Teachers: some are parents, others would like to be parents.

Some are Mr., some are Mrs., and more are Miss. Some are rich, while most are poor. Many have a second job and talk about their other assignment. Others have a second income but cannot talk about it. Some belong to the union, while most play it straight with membership in the local teachers' association, an affiliate of the National Education Association. Some talk about striking and others carry placards in the picket line.

These are the people who teach the nation's children in our public schools. How they teach and what they teach will determine what many of our children think and how they react. In the long run teachers influence the direction our society takes and they determine how this country thinks on critical issues.

Where does the local school superintendent find teachers to handle the myriad of activities in a local school system? Thirty-five years ago and before World War II, a superintendent did not have to leave his office to fill vacancies. There was such a surplus of teachers that many cities refused to employ married women, refused to employ two teachers from the same family, and limited applications to individuals who resided in the local area.

All of this changed in the early fifties. A burgeoning school population, higher salaries in the other professions, and deteriorating conditions in the public schools completely dried up the field and left local school superintendents scurrying about the country and offering contracts to anybody who met minimum state and local credential requirements.

Most of our teachers during the early part of the twentieth century came from teachers' colleges. These institutions, formerly called normal schools, have been treated as poor second cousins by most state legislatures and have had limited finances at their command. They could not compete with the state universities or private colleges and their limited funds resulted in less distinguished faculties, poor buildings, inadequate housing, and lack of equipment. Under these impossible conditions, we trained our teachers. (It would be more accurate to say that we housed our teachers for a period of years, but failed miserably to educate them.) Professors who could not make it at the university level, dormitories that were poorly built and overcrowded, and equipment that was out of pace with our times—this was the setting for the training of our teachers, and the curriculum was in perfect tune with the faculty, the buildings, and the equipment. (These conditions are not unique even now.)

The normal school I attended in New Hampshire, like the state teachers' college I attended in Massachusetts, had a library that was even smaller than our inadequate basement cafeteria and had a relatively small gymnasium that was three times the size of our limited arts and humanities area. Under such intolerable conditions we took predominantly lower middle-class students (generally young people who did not have the financial support to go to the state university or whose high school academic record was such that they could not gain admission to the university) and made them teachers. The people who trained them were usually older, white, Anglo-Saxon. The textbooks they studied were conservative, supporting motherhood and the flag, and designed to perpetuate the society of Harding and Coolidge.

Men were encouraged to major in math and science and vocational education at the secondary level. Women were pushed into primary and elementary education and into the language arts at the high school level. Somehow I managed to break the pattern. I insisted on majoring in elementary education and became the first male to train in one of the training school's first grades. Why? Because I believed we should have males in elementary schools? Oh, no—I wanted a job and openings at the secondary level were practically non-existent.

Conditions have changed. There are fewer "teachers' colleges" now; most of them have become state colleges or universities, but even these are still far from ideal. Despite the fact that we have entered a space age, an age of technology, an age need-

ing astute knowledge and skills in human relations, we continue
to train our teachers in concepts and practices compatible with
pre-World-War-I days.

In 1970 a teacher shortage of major proportion exists in our
country schools, and we have in our schools tens of thousands of
teachers with sub-standard credentials. School superintendents
recruit whatever they can find. Retired military men are prime
prospects for a teaching contract. Former teachers who have
dropped out to raise families are brought back to new classroom
environments without further training. Adults with a degree in
fields other than education are given speedy methods classes and
take over in the classroom.

School superintendents must take all these people and weld
them into an effective team with a common philosophy and with
goals and objectives they can accept. The net result will be
extreme highs and lows, with inconsistency the order of the day.

A school superintendent must develop high esprit de corps at
the staff level and this must start with the respect of the staff for
the superintendent. This can develop only if he is consistent in
his relationship with the teachers. Teachers are told not to play
favorites with children and the same rule holds true for the
superintendent. Consistency and fair play must characterize the
superintendent's relationship with staff.

It is equally important that the staff understand the superintendent's relationship with parents when teachers are involved.
I refuse to be pushed around by a parent or parents who insist
that I intervene for their child in some picayune dispute with a
classroom teacher. Instead, I make it clear to all concerned that
if they have a complaint they should go first to the teacher and
discuss it at that level. Amazingly, most disputes end right there.
Parents frequently discover, on confronting the teacher, that
little Johnny has a very wild imagination and quite often grossly
exaggerates the situation. This procedure results in many parents discovering that the classroom teacher is a reasonable hu-

man being trying desperately to minister to the needs of children under difficult conditions. It also makes the teacher realize that she is being held accountable for her actions but that the superintendent is not being unduly influenced by parents. Above all, it forces the two parties most responsible for a child's education—the teacher and the parents—to talk it over together.

Teachers make mistakes, no more, no less than do doctors and architects. When they make a mistake they should not be publicly embarrassed for their actions. All too often school administrators freely and openly criticize a staff member. There is a time and place for such criticism; but the place is in the privacy of the superintendent's office, and the time is a time convenient for the teacher.

Teachers, because of inadequacies in their educational training, generally need retraining while on the job. The common practice in some school systems has been to require teachers to take specific courses at the close of a school day or on Saturday mornings. The practice of forcing teachers to take these courses on their own time, at the close of a demanding day or after they have worked a full week, must change. Let's give our staff time off during their regular workday or provide a sabbatical leave arrangement for such needed retraining.

Being consistent in action, not over-reacting on behalf of parents, providing reasonable working conditions for the staff and reasonable arrangements for in-service training courses, freeing the teacher to teach, and involving the teacher in decision making—all of these are vital in developing and maintaining staff morale and an effective team.

I know of no better way to turn a teacher and a staff on than to develop a school climate in which teachers feel free and comfortable in their role. This does not mean that the system have no standards, that administration abdicate, or that there be an absence of supervision. On the contrary, it means creative and responsive supervision and clear-cut goals and objectives. The program objectives, however, must be worked out with *total* staff involvement; supervisors, consultants, and coordinators should be selected with staff participation. When we are working toward common goals, when staff participate in selection of their leaders, when clear-cut guide lines are established, then our teachers can be freed so each can do his own thing. We should encourage staff to use their individual and unique talents in a manner that will be satisfying to them. When the teacher is comfortable about what he or she is doing, so are the learners.

A school superintendent can control the quality of education in the local school system by the manner in which he selects his teaching staff. If he wants a system dominated by married women (and many school superintendents feel that this is one way they can control things) then all he has to do is employ a greater number of married women. If he wants a staff that reflects the thinking of the older generation, he holds, for dear life, to the old-timers. If he wants a lily white staff, he tells his board of education that no qualified black, brown, yellow, or red person applied. If he wants to maintain a status quo atmosphere, he screens out candidates from certain liberal schools and picks candidates from colleges with the conservative image.

In Berkeley in the middle and late sixties, in Prince Edward County, and on Long Island before that, I wanted to bring together a staff committed to fostering and encouraging change in our society. I wanted a staff interested in discovering how students learn, in using that knowledge to discover students' interests, and then in providing students with rich experiences in those interest areas. I wanted a staff that would encourage students to challenge textbooks and teachers with critical questions, a staff that accepted individual differences and idiosyncracies, a staff that was not up tight about what a student wore to school or about the length of his hair, a staff that believed in freedom of thought and action, and a staff committed to providing equal educational opportunities to each student.

Could such a staff be found? Yes, indeed. Could they be molded into a cohesive team? You bet! How do I know? Because that is the sort of team I worked with for many years. Oh, they didn't all fall into a single pattern, nor did we agree on all questions. But, by and large, I worked with a tremendously dedicated, talented group of professionals who, despite the inadequacy of their background (mine would be considered by some to be the shabbiest of all), pulled themselves together in one cohesive team.

To create this kind of organization I had to ask some staff members to leave. This is not easy (particularly when some of them had been in the system for as long as fifteen years), but you do not develop a winning team by keeping weaklings in the front line. It has been said by many of my colleagues that you cannot remove an inferior teacher. I admit that it is not easy, but it can be and is done. If a school superintendent is honest with his staff, clearly stating his philosophy and expectations, some staff members will leave without being asked.

Early in my administration in Berkeley, I called the staff together and clearly stated goals for school integration and heterogeneous classes. At that meeting I urged those teachers who did not feel comfortable in a multi-racial situation to go elsewhere and teach. I pointed out that it was a big country and that it wasn't necessary to spend time teaching in an uncomfortable situation. As a result of that speech, those who had respected me before respected me even more, while those who detested me had a clearer picture of me as a superintendent. There was no doubt in anybody's mind about what I expected of them.

Teachers quite often forget why we have schools and need to be reminded that the schools are there for the convenience of the student. Schools are not the property or the plaything of the teacher or the professional staff. I have been disturbed by teachers over the years who lay claim to a particular classroom or a particular school. They become an immovable object, and when an administrator tries to rearrange schedules for the convenience of the students, old Miss Ironsides yells, "No, this is *my* room!"

In 1968 in Berkeley it became necessary to move most of our elementary staff, not only from their old classrooms, but also from their old schools. It was a traumatic experience for many of them but it all worked out beautifully. They discovered that they needed help in the new buildings when they were forced to move around. They suddenly discovered the other fellow, and improved school morale developed.

Morale can be improved in a school system if the superintendent also provides opportunity for staff exposure to the public. Bring to the attention of the board of education unique and creative programs being carried on in the schools and present the staff members responsible. See that meritorious programs are written up in school newsletters and the local newspaper and are featured on radio and television. See that the names and pictures of talented staff members are constantly called to the attention of the total staff and the general public.

School superintendents should give highest priority to improving working conditions. Provide broad health benefits that include everything from dental care to major health benefits. Work to free teachers from the dull bookkeeping, baby-sitting roles, and free them to teach. See that teachers' salaries compare favorably with those of the other professions. Provide a salary schedule that permits outstanding teachers to earn as much as school administrators. Keep class size to a manageable number. All of these things are essential and should be provided to staff without endless hours of debate. All of these things are musts if our teachers are to be effective.

But even if a superintendent provides all of these things, he will not have high staff morale if he fails to encourage an open system of communication with a free flow of ideas and suggestions. Not only must he encourage such a system, but he also must continually develop and nurture it. This system of open communication should begin with the staff meetings held by the superintendent. Classroom teachers should be included as participating members on every district committee. In addition, all meetings should be scheduled in places convenient to teachers (in schools), and, if teachers are free, they should be encouraged to sit in at these sessions.

Newsletters covering all district activities, particularly item-by-item accounts of board of education meetings, are essential—but—a school superintendent is naive if he thinks mimeographed newsletters concerning school activities are sufficient communication between central administration and classroom teachers. He is equally naive if he thinks teachers will come to his office with their suggestions or problems. He must go to them, attend department meetings, and attend some faculty meetings. While it would be impossible for him to touch all the bases in a large school system, he can touch some of them—and he and his fellow administrators working together can touch all of them, if he sets the example.

I learned as a young superintendent in Sanford, Maine, that high morale resulted when staff got to know one another, when primary teachers rubbed elbows with the foreign language and math teachers at the secondary level on a project that had meaning to them. We structured our meetings on a vertical basis—small groups of teachers and administrators meeting one week in a kindergarten, the next week in a high school science lab, and the following week in an art room at one of the junior high schools. It was a productive period in curriculum development, but even more important, the staff became better acquainted. They had to cope together with curriculum problems and people problems and this developed an outstanding faculty.

The Sanford experience paid rich dividends to those of us who went to Virginia in the summer of 1963, at President Kennedy's request, to open the Free Schools for the black children of Prince Edward County. I seized every opportunity to bring that staff together. We had gathered from across the country—black and white, young and old, Peace Corps veterans and army rejects, from small rural schools and from New York City, some garrulous, others afraid to open their mouths. I had only a few weeks to prepare the staff for the returning students, so we used every working hour, seven days a week, to accomplish the task.

Some local factors were a blessing in disguise. Our mixed group could not attend the local theater or the white Protestant churches, or go to the hotel or to the restaurants; so we stuck together, ate in one or two locations, and fought the local police when one of our staff was falsely arrested. We became one great, strong, effective school family. And how this rubbed off on our action in the classroom! The students recognized our cohesiveness, parents quickly got the message, and the most effective teaching I have ever observed took place. We not only worked together and fought together but we also played together. I arranged evening activities throughout the year. The students, faculty, and parents had one big party with dancing, plenty of food, groovy music, and good fellowship.

I hope that never again do conditions occur in this country that will force a President to open "free schools" for deprived children, but I do wish that the spirit of the Prince Edward County faculty could be recaptured by teachers in every nook and corner of this country.

6

Parents and PTAs

Harper Valley Not Necessary

Parents: they too come in all shapes and sizes. I have come to admire and respect them. They blow up when life for their child becomes difficult. And why not? They remain silent when their child's report card is covered with A's and E's. And why not? They rarely come to board of education meetings held in the late evenings far from their homes. And why should they, particularly when the agenda remains a big, dark secret? They seldom attend PTA meetings. And why should they? Such meetings rarely discuss critical problems facing the school; unfortunately, they turn into afternoon gossip sessions. (Did the Harper Valley PTA recording become a number one hit because Jeannie Riley has such an enticing voice, or because conditions in the Harper Valley PTA were altogether too realistic and the general public identified with the people Jeannie described?)

They don't get excited about school board elections, because the establishment's candidates have things nicely tied up long before election day. They rarely visit the school superintendent's office, because the welcome sign is not to be found in most central offices. (Why do some school secretaries over-protect their bosses from parents?)

The parent who generally appears at school is Mommy, not Daddy. Of course, Father may be too busy, but educators also tend to develop a climate that attracts women and discourages men. We hold our meetings in the afternoons after school, or we constantly hold luncheon meetings for parents. A few years ago in Long Island I decided to try a different approach with parents. We arranged breakfast meetings beginning at 7:00 A.M.—designed for dads—and we were amazed at the results. The dads came in large numbers, practically all of them. At this breakfast meeting we made more points for the school and public education than we had ever made at an afternoon tea or luncheon for mothers.

Parents: are they represented by the parent-teacher associations? I don't believe it. Parents are not really organized at all. If they were, conditions in our schools would be different—more pupil oriented and less teacher oriented.

I recall addressing my first PTA meeting in my second superintendency in 1950 in Springvale, Maine. The meeting started at 7:30 P.M. with the traditional flag ceremonies, treasurer's report, the secretary's report, a check on parents present to see which room won the attendance plaque, old business, committee reports, and then new business. I was to speak following new business. At 9:45 P.M. they were still discussing what they would have for refreshments at the next meeting and whether or not they should spend $6.50, of the $14.91 remaining in the treasury, for new coffee cups (to be used once a month at PTA meetings).

I almost blew my superintendency that evening. I was angry and, unfortunately, when I am angry I show it to all present. I pointed out that we had spent an entire evening discussing such topics as coffee cups and whether or not they should have a ventriloquist at the next meeting. The entire evening had slipped away while the Superintendent of Schools waited. The Superintendent had started his day at 6:00 A.M. assessing the weather to see if conditions were safe to operate school buses. He had continued for sixteen hours without any break, and now, at 10:00 P.M., they finally got around to asking him to speak.

They got more than they bargained for. I told them that I was angry (surprise), and I told them precisely why. While they were discussing the critical situation of coffee cups needed for PTA meetings, they never did get around to discussing the over-crowded conditions in grade two (forty-five students and one teacher), the lack of a library or library facilities, an inadequate playground, a principal who had a full teaching load, two perma-nent substitute teachers, the lack of a 16–mm projector, the one broken slide projector, or the 75 percent of the students carrying cold lunches to school because there was no provision for a hot lunch program! (I must say they were tolerant, appreciative, understanding, and helpful, once the problems were called to their attention.)

Parents talk about coffee cups and refreshments for PTA meetings because too often a school superintendent wants to keep them from interfering. "Give them busy work," an old-timer told me. "That will keep them out of your hair." It surely will. It will also develop a school system that merely exists, where nothing new happens, where children figuratively dry up and die, and where creative teachers who do come in get out as fast as they can.

Parents and PTAs have been exploited by many school princi-pals and school superintendents. I recall hearing a school super-intendent of one of our largest cities tell an assembled group of school administrators that he based his success on his ability to keep all important questions and issues away from parents and board of education members. He pointed out that he would ask interested groups to decide such vital questions as where the school cafeteria manager should buy the bread for the school kitchens. Is it any wonder, once this pinhead left and a new superintendent was employed, that all hell broke loose when parents were given an opportunity to appraise, realistically, conditions in their schools?

Those Springvale parents taught me a most important lesson: give them a chance to be involved with the real problems. Report the strong points of the system, but call the weaknesses to their attention as well. Join *with* them in developing goals and objectives. Price out these goals. Set priorities. And then ask the parents to form the team to convince the entire community of the needs. Then *they* will sell a tax election successfully in their district.

I made few points with PTA leaders in Berkeley in 1964 when I met them for the first time. I made it clear that I did not intend to wet nurse them, that I intended to involve *all* of the parents not *some* of the parents, that every taxpayer was equally important, that my home was my castle, and that I did not intend to hold small group PTA meetings in my living room.

Again, they were tolerant and understanding of the new flamboyant school superintendent. A few became angry and never got over it; but to their everlasting credit they joined me in attacking the unequal educational opportunities in the system and, together, we changed the system and developed one that observers called worthy of imitation. They proved to be great supporters of public education—once they recognized that they could be full partners in improving the system.

But the secret of a successful school system is to involve all of the parents, not some of them. How to do it: that is the important question. The answer, of course, depends upon the man, the people, and the students. Many different approaches have been successful but I can report first hand only those techniques which have succeeded with me. Basically, the best approach is to bring the parents together with the child's teacher. Get the parents when they and their children are young; involve them early, during the child's first three or four years in school. Make the parents knowledgeable about weaknesses as well as strengths, and develop in them a desire and, indeed, an eagerness to come to school, to visit the child's teacher, and to chat about what goes on in the classroom.

Encourage individual classroom teachers to hold their own meetings for parents of children in the classroom. Hold these meetings at various times: early morning, noontime, rarely in the evening. The teacher also should go to the home of the child. This is more important than the parent coming to the school. Face to face meetings—that is the way to get dialogue going, to win support for education, and, even more important, to get individual parents, the child, and the teacher together under the *child's roof* where parent and child are comfortable. Together they can zero in on what is happening to the child and decide how the school can help.

I recall my first year as a classroom teacher in the White Mountains of New Hampshire: my annual salary of $800, the number of students (forty-eight first through eighth graders), the lack of supplies and equipment, the extremely cold weather, and the difficulties we had with a pot-bellied stove when the temperature dropped to 40° below zero. But we were a close family and we worked together. Why? The parents and the children knew the teacher. Circumstances probably forced us together, but whatever the catalyst was, we should rediscover and imitate it in our schools today.

I recall being invited to a different home twice a week for the evening meal and to spend the hours before bedtime with the family. Sometimes we played games; some evenings there was a songfest; at times we studied the map or discussed such important questions as the school's chemical toilet or the condition of the school well. We got to know one another—the parents and the child and the teacher—under ideal conditions.

The experience in that mountain community convinced me of the need for parent-teacher meetings and communications. I have used every technique imaginable to develop this in our schools, and I know it can be done. Take report cards. The formal report card should be eliminated. In its place we should require parent-teacher-student conferences. Hold one in the school, the next one in the home. Free the teacher from regular classroom assignments and train her in the techniques of teacher-parent conferences. Emphasize the important items: the attitude of the child toward learning and toward his peers. Is he making progress, or just marking time? Is he measuring up to his innate ability? What about his willingness to help others? There are so many things perceptive teachers can measure and report besides the child's skill in mathematics and science.

Stop giving parents busy work such as handing out napkins at school parties. Bring them closer to the schools and into the mainstream of vital ongoing school activities. Although it was started before my arrival, I point with pride to the success of the School Resources Volunteers in Berkeley in helping to accomplish this. Here is a project that is indeed meritorious and worthy of imitation.

It all begins with the classroom teacher; he identifies areas in the regular classroom program where he could use help. He might ask for assistance in tutoring the slow learner, or in helping to enrich the curriculum for the high potential student. He might ask for help to plan and carry out a field trip to the local post office or to some other point of interest in the community. Help could mean the involvement of a parent skilled in the medium of modern art or jazz. But above all, it brings parent and teacher together in ministering to the needs of young children.

And it does much more than that. It demonstrates to the child that parents and teacher are partners in the learning-teaching situation, that school is not an isolated island but an integral part of the total family of parents, children, school, and community.

School superintendents should not only encourage parent-teacher relationships, but should also structure situations to bring the teacher and community together in common efforts to understand and improve conditions in the public schools. Do not wait for this to happen; personally request the board of education to name ad hoc committees; confront parents and taxpayers and teachers and urge them to address themselves to the problems of the city schools.

Dialogue—that is what is needed. Confrontation—that is what is needed. Confrontation of parents and teachers in reasonable situations. From this will come understanding and appreciation of the roles both parents and teachers must play in building a school program that will meet the needs of all children who attend our public schools.

Relationships can work out when the respective parties are not threatened by each other's presence. I readily admit that in some cases (paranoid teacher, overzealous parent) it just cannot work out. But in most cases, a teacher will welcome parents' help when the ground rules for their involvement are spelled out and agreed upon by those involved. Parent-teacher relationships should develop naturally. Parents cannot be forced on teacher or teacher on parents.

Many of my evenings have been spoiled by parents who insist on getting to the man on top regarding a situation involving their child and his school. I have been reasonably successful in directing them to the school, the teacher involved, and the principal, but many a time I have taken the brunt of the attack. I would like the record to show that those particular parents are most often those who have been brain washed by their darling sons or daughters. "Conned" is a better way of putting it (not always, but generally).

I recall in Berkeley being torn into by a parent who was irate over the school principal who, according to Daddy, forced his child to go out on the playground during a heavy rain storm. Johnny had not told it the way it really happened. As a matter of fact, there had not been a recess period at all that day. Instead

Johnny had gotten wet by voluntarily getting off the school bus so he could visit a friend on the way to school!

Children have vivid imaginations and are great story tellers. Parents should realize this, and also should realize that kids, just like adults, tend to exaggerate. I am not saying that teachers do not occasionally take advantage of a child, but, by and large, teachers are consistent and tolerant and do everything humanly possible to follow school rules. Their behavior, more often than not, is highly ethical. But, all too often, gullible parents believe whatever little Janie tells them, and either draw false conclusions about the teacher and the school, or attack innocent classroom teachers and administrators.

Neither the parent nor the school can bring up and educate a child alone. They must talk to each other, compare notes, call each other's attention to things each should know about the child. The best way to do this is through formal and informal meetings arranged either by the school or the parent, preferably with the school taking the initiative.

When teacher and parent meet, relate to one another, and interact, many interesting situations occur. In the late fifties I employed the first black teacher in the schools of East Williston on Long Island. His name was Edgar Thomas and he was a thoroughly outstanding individual. After his first year on the faculty at the Wheatley School, I named him to the top position in that department, Curriculum Associate.

Ed was the type of teacher who creeps up on students and suddenly has them all eating out of his hand. He was quiet, had a warm outgoing personality, could smile easily, and knew his field extremely well. The students (including my two sons, Roger and Michael) fell head over heels in love with him. When I nominated Edgar Thomas for the position, one W.A.S.P. member of the Board of Education asked me why I was nominating a Negro. I casually replied that: a) he was the best qualified candidate and b) it was about time white suburban districts made an all-out effort to have minority members on the professional staff. He didn't press his question and, as a matter of record, Mr. Thomas was unanimously elected.

But how did parents react? We had open house activities during American Education Week in November and I attended, both as a parent and as the local superintendent. I was scheduled, along with the other parents, to follow one of our son's regular programs. In the third period we left Roger's foreign language class and obediently moved on to advanced science. I arrived first, said hello to Mr. Thomas, and then observed the mothers and dads as they entered the room. To say that they were surprised would not adequately describe the reaction of a majority of parents. Shock would be a better word. Later in the evening several of them came to me and expressed their appreciation for my bringing a black teacher into the district. The same message came through over and over again: "Dr. Sullivan, we knew Tommy's (or Jane's) teacher's name was Mr. Thomas, but we never expected him to be black. Why didn't Tom (or Jane) tell us?"

Well, mothers and dads, you see, young people do not have the same hang-ups over race as our generation has (unless you brainwashed them). Young people, if left to their own devices, will appraise a teacher on his ability to teach and on his ability to relate to them in an open, positive fashion. If he is a competent teacher, they couldn't care less about his color, religion, political conviction, or how he combs his hair.

Something about teenagers and how they report school news to parents needs to be understood. Most junior and senior high school students report very little to parents. They don't want parents visiting school, talking to their teacher or to the school administration. As a result, parents have a difficult time finding out how well their children are getting along. It is important that parents respect the position their adolescent offspring take on visiting school, but they must find some ways of tuning in on

school activities of their children. Here, the school should provide the ways and means! The best way, of course, is to have
guidance workers and counselors in large enough numbers to
counsel students and still have sufficient scheduled time to meet
with each parent several times during the year. If a student is
running into difficulty the counselor should communicate directly with the parents at once.

As Berkeley's Superintendent of Schools in the middle sixties,
I was concerned about the rising incidence of drug and narcotics
use by some young people. My staff brought in a competent
researcher who carefully studied what was going on, and then
gave us the facts. The facts were shockingly bad. He found that
we were living in an area where drugs were readily available, and
that conditions in our shcools were no better or worse than in
other Bay Area high schools. We moved immediately to provide
the finest instruction available on the dangers of using narcotics.
We carefully evaluated the course—did thorough and constant
research. After two years, despite our Herculean efforts, the use
of drugs had increased slightly.

It became perfectly clear to me that the schools alone could
not solve the problem. We needed a total community effort. We
needed parents who were knowledgeable about drug effects and
parents who could recognize the early symptoms of drug use by
their children. So, we turned to the parents and encouraged
them to enroll in the new courses we introduced on the subject
of drugs, courses designed for teachers and parents. Record
numbers of adults enrolled in the courses and the reaction of
parents was most gratifying. I'm not sure how great an impact
the adult courses had on student use of narcotics. But if we
helped one parent with one child, the effort was worthwhile.

I have strong feelings about parental responsibility for being
knowledgeable about such subjects as the use of drugs and home
and family living (including sex education). I am proud to report
that in the 1960s I introduced these courses in public schools

under my supervision, and to the everlasting credit of the people in these districts, the courses have been accepted with broad community support. Why were they accepted in city A and fought in city B? I am not absolutely certain about community B, but I can tell you why parents did not oppose the courses in city A. They were first exposed to the problem, and then were involved in structuring the courses. In addition, a careful curriculum was planned and built by experts in the field, the staff was carefully selected, proper materials and equipment were provided for the staff, the program was carefully evaluated several times each semester by staff, students, and parents, and revisions were made when weaknesses were revealed.

In discussing parents, two pet shibboleths should be noted. The first is that parents will not support innovation in a school system. I cannot accept this belief commonly held by school superintendents. We closed one-room schools in rural Maine with the support of parents. We combined grades in Sanford, Maine, putting third and fourth graders in the same room, with the approval of parents. We introduced a completely non-graded system in the elementary schools on Long Island without real opposition from parents. We held school on Saturdays in Prince Edward County. Parents applauded. In Berkeley, we changed a 7-8-9 grade junior high school (the first in the United States, 1917) to a 7-8 grade combination and put all the ninth graders on a central campus. We broke down at the secondary level a tight teaching system that had existed for over forty years. We moved an elementary system that had been organized as K-6 neighborhood schools to a K-3 (primary school), 4-6 (middle school) organization. We bused children who had never been bused before. We moved white middle class children into black ghetto schools.

"We" did it is the way it should be said—we, the parents, we, the staff, we, the students, and we, the community, Careful planning? You bet! Skillful selling? Of course. Careful consideration of the whole community? You are so right. Lots of meetings? Hundreds of meetings. Lots of publicity? Tons of publicity. Any opposition? Lots of opposition in the initial stages but little opposition at the end. Outside experts used to sell the program? Certainly not! All the talent we needed was right there in the community, and on the staff.

We successfully moved the new programs because we believed that they were all educationally sound and legally right. We worked with the total community, educating them on the strength of the new concepts. Did we wait until we were absolutely certain that we had parental consensus? No. When the staff was ready and when we had carefully involved the total community, we moved on the new program. I cannot see waiting until you are certain that consensus exists. How does one ever know when that exact time arrives? If we had waited for a consensus on slavery, we would still have slaves! Do your work carefully, but do not delay once the staff is ready; and, of course, once the new programs are introduced, evaluate them every step of the way. No, I have not found that parents object to new and innovative programs in our public schools.

The second shibboleth is that parents want to control the schools. Let us first set the record straight—parents *do* control the schools. Who, after all, is on our boards of education and our school committees? Who elects these people? Parents, that's who. Remember, the schools belong to the people.

However, I realize that a school superintendent must not relinquish his professional leadership to small or large pressure groups who have an axe to grind. I have been tested by such groups. If the top administrator vacillates or abdicates, a vacuum occurs and whoever is strongest takes over. It could be parents; it could be teachers; every once in a while it is the students. But, again, let us set the record straight. These groups take over only when weak and inefficient leadership exists on the central administrative staff. If the superintendent, in his professional opinion, finds that the objectives of such groups are narrow, selfish, and not in the best interests of freedom in our schools, he should challenge and fight them at every turn. The school administrator should demonstrate courage and provide leadership to the staff, the students, the parents, and the community so that all can work together to create an effective school system.

Before wrapping up this chapter on parents let us look for a moment at those early years of the child and his relationship to his parents, to his school, and to his teacher. The average young child loves school, adores his teacher, and wants to share his experience with those he loves, particularly other members of the family. Let us take advantage of these beautiful years. Visit school often. Invite the teacher to visit your home. Take the younger members of the family with you when you go to school. Invite the neighbor next door (he pays taxes too, you know). Encourage your child to talk about school and listen when he does.

While parents have this beautiful opportunity awaiting them, the school also has a golden opportunity to sell public education to parents. Children should be coached—yes, coached—by their teachers at the end of each day on what happened in school that day. Young minds have short memories. Unless the child is reminded at the close of the day about what took place during this school day, the following is apt to happen at the dinner table at 6:00 P.M.

DADDY: "And what did you do in school today, Roddy?"

RODDY: "Nothing."

7

Evaluation

Springboard for Improvement

On an October Saturday morning in 1957, newspaper head-lines screamed out the news of the Russian conquest of outer space. The launching of the first Sputnik was instantly recog-nized as a great achievement, a great step forward for mankind in the conquest of our environment. However, for an American nation accustomed over its 200-year history to "winning," this represented a tremendous blow to prestige. This achievement had been gained by another nation; America had been "de-feated" in the race to place an object in orbit around the earth. We immediately began to look for scapegoats, and public educa-tion became a focus of criticism. American education has not been the same since!

Had the Russians beaten us into outer space because our public schools had failed to educate the scientists needed to get us there first? There were demagogues aplenty who complained about the alleged laxness in public school standards after World War II. They now had a field day, ignoring the fact that most of the scientists working in the space program may have had their public school education considerably earlier than the period of alleged laxness. Furthermore, could the people who took this opportunity to criticize the shortcomings of public education legitimately hide the fact that in almost every category, other than the race into space, America led the world in technological development? However, rightly or wrongly, the launching of Sputnik led to a critical scrutiny of public schools in America; and, although I reject the validity of the cause, I regard this new look at American education as a positive development. It stimulated a renewed interest in our schools and a greater concern that our students be well educated.

However, some of this interest took hysterical forms. In many communities, gifted students were isolated from their peers and given crash programs on technological subjects such as mathematics and science. I have no quarrel with developing programs to encourage gifted students to realize their full potential. But this cannot be done in isolation from other students and it cannot be done in such a way as to neglect the education of others. Both science and mathematics are extremely important subjects, but they cannot be allowed to dominate the curriculum to the extent that students are under-educated in the humanities and the arts. Unfortunately, this was the result in too many instances in the immediate post-Sputnik era.

Another attribute of the post-Sputnik era was a demand that an approved way be found for evaluating education. Proponents of standardized tests had a field day. In some states, including California, massive programs of mandated state tests at various grade levels were introduced. People were searching for ways of determining whether or not their school systems were doing a good job.

This new emphasis on evaluation generally represented a positive development in education. The public had been too long content with leaving education to the educators. Parents and other taxpayers remained both under-informed and under-interested in what took place behind the walls of the local public schools. Although there were exceptions in every community, the prevailing mood prior to Sputnik was indifference, and this mood was encouraged by many members of our profession. Too frequently, we reacted to efforts to evaluate our work by using the cop-out that the education of a child was such an intangible thing and occurred so gradually over so long a period of time and under such a wide variety of stimulants that it was impossible adequately to measure any single factor in that growth. The public, already beginning to chafe under this kind of evasion, refused to accept it any longer after Sputnik. If educators could not come up with reasonable methods of evaluation, the public would do it for them! (In some instances, such as the California testing program, that is exactly what happened.) Many school systems did recognize this need and began to develop organized programs for evaluating their work.

EVALUATION OF STAFF PERSONNEL

No school system is better than the caliber of its instructional staff. Although many elements must go into a successful school system, the people who have a direct impact on the instructional program are of foremost concern and must be selected with great care. In fact, decisions concerning the selection of instructional personnel are among the most crucial any superintendent must make. Also, decisions on whether or not to retain personnel from year to year, particularly when these decisions involve tenure, represent a vital portion of a superintendent's role. He must have a sound system of personnel evaluation that covers those who have tenure and those who do not, as well as those who are the subject of consideration for placement within the system. No superintendent who takes his job seriously can leave this part of it to chance.

However, when we think of personnel evaluation we think too often in the narrow context of hire-fire decisions. Although such decisions are important, personnel evaluation should also serve the equally important purpose of providing a springboard for improvement. We must instill in our colleagues evaluative attitudes that will cause us to constantly ask questions such as, "Who am I reaching? Who am I failing to reach? What am I doing that is successful? And where do I need improvement?" We need both types of evaluation—that which serves as a guide for decisions regarding employment status and that which serves as the springboard for improvement. Neither can be left to chance.

Let's consider first the more commonly accepted concept of evaluation, that for hire-fire purposes. Until very recently decisions regarding who was a good teacher and who was not were based primarily on skill in maintaining classroom discipline. I have even heard of one principal who regularly told the new members of his teaching staff that one way to judge their effectiveness was by looking at the floor near the end of the day. If there were many paperwads on the floor this was an indication that the teacher was not particularly effective that day and that the students were presumably not sufficiently inspired to refrain from throwing paperwads. The effect of that principal's comment was predictable. The teacher simply would make it his business to be sure that the paperwads were picked up before the janitor came in to sweep at the close of the day. The janitor might be, in effect, evaluating their teaching. As a means of lightening the janitor's work, this was effective. As a means of evaluation, self or otherwise, it was not. Other principals based their opinion of teachers on the number of youngsters who were sent to the office. In many instances, criteria such as these would be the only basis that a principal would have for evaluation, since he did not personally come near the classroom while the class was in session. The principal's role was seen as a combination of shop foreman and plant manager who simply passed out the textbooks, scheduled the teacher into the room, and judged the teacher as good or bad depending upon whether or not the teacher "made waves"—either through being unable to handle the class or through being a personal "troublemaker."

Fortunately, this type of supervision was rejected in most places years ago. More recently principals have given at least lip-service to the need to get into classrooms to engage in personal observations. However, in too many cases, principals still do not know what to look for once they enter a classroom. If they are not there often enough to catch the context of a given lesson, their observations tend toward noting room temperature, exhibits on the board, and other such things. Sincere as many of these efforts have been, they simply have not been adequate to determine a teacher's effectiveness. The usual result was that if a teacher survived the probationary period, maintained reasonable classroom decorum, got along reasonably well with other members of the faculty, and did not "make waves," he could be pretty certain that he would receive tenure. In most instances, that was the last evaluation he saw.

The history of administrative evaluation has been even more shocking. Until recent years, too many school districts have had "royal principals." Each principal was royal within his own domain, right or wrong, competent or incompetent. The central administration would feel it necessary to back each principal in order to maintain the authority of the system as a whole. In this kind of an arrangement, there was no incentive for local building principals to be particularly creative or to continue their professional growth. All that was necessary was for them to operate their buildings in such a way as to cause a minimum of disturbance "downtown."

This kind of staff evaluation will no longer suffice. If our schools are to do the job expected of them, they must have top personnel and these personnel must perform to the best of their capabilities. You will have neither result unless our personnel evaluation is strong enough to bring these conditions about.

Three bases must be touched in setting up an evaluation program: criteria, agent, and methodology. Since an evaluation program depends upon its acceptance both by persons being

evaluated and by any persons who are asked to believe the results, it is important that all three of these dimensions be understood and accepted by everyone concerned. Teachers and
administrators alike should be involved in planning the program.

The criteria vary from place to place and from time to time.
Although the details covered and the exact wording vary, most
lists of criteria cover the following areas: knowledge of subject
matter or special area of expertise; understanding of, and ability
to relate to, students; skill and techniques of teaching; ability to
maintain an atmosphere that is conducive to learning; participation as a team member of the total school staff; ability to relate
well to parents and other members of the community and to be
a satisfactory representative of the school; and the broad, rather
nebulous area of "personal" characteristics. The last should include only those things that have a direct impact on fulfilling the
role. Time and energy should not be wasted in needless battles
over personal tastes in dress, grooming, and other such trivia.
However, such personal characteristics as promptness, acceptance of responsibility, and dependability are essential elements
of success in virtually every school situation.

The question of who does the evaluating can be a sticky one.
This is generally accepted to be an administrative role, at least,
where evaluation for tenure or for continued employment is
concerned. This can be satisfactory when the administrator himself is competent and qualified to perform the evaluation needed.
However, we should not be afraid to experiment with new ways
of doing things. We need to come up with systems of evaluation
that involve many others in the process. This is particularly true
of the evaluation that is not related to job retention, but rather
to improving the effectiveness of the person under evaluation.

Teacher organizations frequently can be of help. It has been
my experience, particularly in recent years, that teacher organization leadership is both keenly aware of the need for good
evaluation and willing to participate in establishing it. Far from
opposing programs of teacher evaluation, these leaders have ex-

pressed to me the feeling that they, too, have a stake in making sure that the profession as a whole performs as well as possible. This means that each member in the profession must be performing at his maximum. It means further that people who are totally ineffective as teachers should not be protected from the kind of evaluation which might indicate this incompetence. Since both the administration and the members of the teaching staff have indicated by their vocational choices that they are keenly interested in each child receiving a good education, both groups have a vital stake in seeing that personnel evaluation is effective and meaningful.

In addition to helping develop a program of evaluation, teachers frequently can be helpful in implementing it. Teachers can be assigned to serve on committees set up to evaluate the work of other teachers. I feel that each teacher should undergo periodic review and evaluation by such a committee of peers. Only in extreme cases would this kind of evaluation be concerned with job termination. The normal function of this kind of evaluation would simply be to help the teacher improve in effectiveness. With this kind of emphasis no teacher need feel threatened by regular evaluation by peers.

If there is a clear understanding of the criteria of the person(s) doing the evaluation and of the methodology for evaluation, the evaluation program itself can be a uniting, rather than a dividing, force. More important, it can be a positive aid in improving the effectiveness of all staff members.

EVALUATION OF STUDENTS

Student evaluation has not been neglected to the same degree as staff evaluation, but it still leaves much to be desired. Often it seems that there are as many different systems of student evaluation as there are teachers on the staff. Some teachers are highly subjective and base their evaluation of student progress strictly on opinion. These opinions are almost invariably affected by the student's manners, appearance, and background, even though this influence is often subconscious. At the other extreme, we find the teacher who carries the long division to the fourth decimal point when figuring the youngster's grade average. Both extremes are wrong.

As in the case with staff evaluation, there needs to be a clear understanding of the criteria on which student achievement is being judged. This will vary from subject to subject within the curriculum. Some subject areas lend themselves more readily to objective evaluation than do others. However, in all instances, the criteria need to be clearly understood and need to bear a direct relationship to the importance of the activity under evaluation in the growth and development of the child.

In any discussion of evaluation one of the issues which must be resolved is the role played by standardized tests. Attitudes toward this type of test vary from an uncritical acceptance of results as valid indicators of the success of the person or program being tested to an almost complete rejection of standardized tests as having any validity at all. The truth lies between these extremes.

Reliance on standardized tests as the sole indicators of quality poses real dangers. Material measured by standardized tests must be reducible to relatively objective test items. Not all subjects or areas of education lend themselves to this approach. The development of attitudes, appreciations, and personal standards, as well as certain skills, cannot be successfully tested through this medium. Dependence upon standardized tests implies that aspects of the curriculum which do not lend themselves readily to such testing are somehow less important as functions of public education. Furthermore, too great a reliance on standardized tests as the determiner of educational quality or success can lead teachers to "teach to the test"—to emphasize those items that are apt to appear on this kind of test.

Another danger of standardized tests is the misuse which can result in oversimplifying "cause and effect" relationships. Education is a complex business. Results on a given test can be caused by many variables; whether a student slept well the night before, whether he panics with paper and pencil tests, whether he feels that the effort of the test is worthwhile, all can affect his score as much as whether or not he really has mastered the material being tested.

There are, of course, positive uses of standardized tests. Such tests can provide valuable clues as to whether or not certain aspects of the program are succeeding. Taken on a mass basis they can reveal areas that need to be given more attention or approaches that need to be changed. In the case of individual students, such tests can be used, in combination with other clues, for the development of a profile indicating strengths and weaknesses of student achievement. They can also assist in helping the student to plan future courses of action. I am not advocating that standardized tests be abandoned or abolished but rather that they should not be misused. In the vernacular of the courtroom, standardized tests should be regarded as witnesses, not judge and jury.

CONCLUSION

Evaluation has been one of the most neglected aspects of education. Because of this lack of adequate evaluation, programs have been perpetuated far beyond their utility, people have been kept in positions for which they are manifestly unsuited, and students have been permitted to go through our school systems without receiving the help that is their birthright. Meanwhile, expenses of education have continued to soar. Our citizens are rightfully demanding an accounting of what their taxes are buying. They will not long continue to pay ever-increasing taxes without evaluation that will assure them that the money is being well spent. It is urgent that educators develop systems of evaluation that will lead to improvements in our performance and will assure our patrons that the schools are doing the best job possible.

8

The Public Schools and Religion

Separation With Cooperation

Being a Catholic and a public school educator, one of the first questions I am usually asked when accepting a new position is, "How do you feel about separation of Church and State and its effect on schools?" Since my church operates an extensive parochial school network, the question is a natural one, and I do not mind answering over and over again. My record should speak for itself. I have devoted my entire professional career to the public schools. I have a personal commitment to public school education and to the separation of Church and State.

I firmly believe, as do most modern educators, that the public schools should not be used to further the interest of one religious group over another. Any public institution which serves and belongs to a pluralistic society must maintain neutrality among that society's various religious communities.

In the First Amendment to the Constitution of the United States the statement "Congress shall make no law respecting an establishment of religion or prohibiting the free exercise thereof . . ." sets the tone for this posture of religious neutrality in government or government agencies. However, the effect of this statement on various types of activities within public schools has

been the subject of differing opinions and of considerable litiga-
tion almost since the founding of this country. One extreme
argues that this phrase is irrelevant to the public schools, that it
speaks to the question of whether or not the government should
establish one church as the "official" church of the nation (e.g.
Church of England). The other extreme uses this constitutional
amendment to forbid any mention in the public school program
of religion, or religious beliefs or customs. Most educators, including myself, stand somewhere between these extremes in
their interpretation.

These differences of opinion are clearly illustrated in the different practices followed in schools, and in some of the rules that
have governed the schools during the nearly two centuries of our
nation's existence. In many of our Eastern states and in many
rural areas it was a common practice until recent years for local
ministers to take turns conducting a weekly chapel service in the
high school. Many states have had laws directing that prayers
and Bible reading be a regular part of the school's program. This,
of course, runs into the difficulty, in a multi-religious society, of
reaching agreement on what should be contained in the prayers
or in the Bible readings. In view of the many different religious
views prevalent in any given community, the prospects for not
offending somebody's religious sensitivities are virtually nil.
Sometimes there is flagrant imposition of one favorite view upon
those who disagree; sometimes attempts are made to reach a
common denominator among the various religious persuasions.
The latter course generally results in something so insipid that
it has the opposite effect from the one intended. In my opinion,
one of the most ludicrous attempts to bring devotional exercises
into the school curriculum and yet not offend anybody was the
so-called Regents' Prayer adopted in the state of New York. This
is the prayer: "Almighty God, we acknowledge our dependence
upon Thee, and we beg Thy blessing upon us, our parents, our
teachers and our country." Now, I am not taking issue with the

sentiments of this prayer. But the idea that anyone is going to be made more religious simply by repeating it day after day is patently absurd, particularly when the prayer is mandated. In fact, rote repetition of such a prayer could inoculate youngsters permanently against a genuine religious experience.

This particular prayer was challenged in the courts as a violation of the First Amendment to the Constitution. Although the New York state courts upheld the state's power to use the Regents' Prayer, these rulings were reversed by the United States Supreme Court.

In another landmark decision relating to two cases—one from Pennsylvania; one from Maryland—the Supreme Court in 1963 ruled that reading of the Bible and recitation of the Lord's Prayer during daily opening exercises in the public schools were unconstitutional. In the majority opinion Mr. Justice Clark stated:

> The place of religion in our society is an exalted one, achieved through a long tradition of reliance on the home, the church, the inviolable citadel of the individual heart and mind. We have come to recognize through bitter experience that it is not within the power of Government to invade that citadel, whether its purpose or effect be to aid or oppose, to advance or retard the relationship between man and religion. The State is firmly committed to a position of neutrality. While the application of that rule requires interpretation of a delicate sort, the rule itself is clearly and concisely stated in the words of the First Amendment.

Although the ruling in these cases struck down the use of Bible reading and the Lord's Prayer during regular school exercises, the majority of concurring opinions made it clear that this rule did not restrict the non-devotional use of the Bible in the public schools nor did it prevent the teaching *about* religion as distinguished from the teaching *of* religion, or recitation by public school children from historical documents which contained references to the Deity. In other words, the schools cannot sponsor exercises that can be interpreted as religiously devotional in nature nor can they sponsor overt acts of worship. However, many conservative religious leaders to the contrary, this Supreme Court ruling does not remove the Bible, in particular, nor religion, in general, from the schools. The Bible may be taught as literature and as a historic document which has had a tremendous impact upon the development of Western civilization. The role which religion has played in the history of man, the role which it plays in human lives, and the role which religious institutions play in the community today are all legitimate areas for coverage in the school curriculum. Likewise, students may study about the various beliefs and customs of different religious communities.

In contrast to the thinking of some religious leaders, I feel that these guidelines by the Supreme Court greatly increase the chances of meaningful treatment of religion as a subject in our schools. The only restrictions have been against the devotional use of religion and the inculcation of a preference for one religion over another. The schools cannot do a competent job of the former and would do violence to one of the cornerstones of American democracy if it attempted the latter. However, by including the role which religion has played in history, literature, art, and society, schools can greatly increase the students' understanding of the effect that religion has had on the history of mankind. In short, the school cannot do the job of the church, temple, or synagogue, nor should it attempt to take over that job.

RELIGIOUS HOLIDAYS

Our schools confront the topic of religion perhaps most dramatically in the way they treat religious holidays. In spite of national protestations of neutrality among religious sects, there has been a long history of one-sidedness in our schools as well as in our society.

The Christmas holidays represent the longest single break in the academic year. During the weeks preceding Christmas, Christian symbols, songs, drama, tableaux, and the like, are frequently a prominent, even a dominant part of the instructional program. This is not surprising in view of the overwhelming deference which our society gives to the Christmas season compared with other religious holidays. However, this represents an emphasis on one religion over others. Furthermore, it frequently places the child of a different religion in an awkward position. He often must decide whether or not to participate in Christian pageants, sing Christmas carols, or take part in other activities of the Christmas season. Although in most instances today he is not compelled to take part in these activities, still, his declining to do so singles him out as different from those who do. This is unfair.

Does this mean that we should throw Christmas out of the curriculum? Of course not! The study of religious holidays, particularly those that have special meaning to the major religious communities of our society, is an important part of education. It is possible to study the traditions which many religious groups have placed about their various holidays without putting a youngster in a position of having to join in a devotional exercise. It goes without saying that the same treatment should be given major holidays of all major religions represented in this society. Since the schools are dismissed on Christmas and Good Friday, non-Christian students should have the right to be excused from school for their religious holidays, and if the numbers involved are substantial, the schools should be shut down for those religious holidays as well.

Early in my superintendency in Berkeley, I received many letters from members of the local Jewish congregation and was visited by the rabbi. The thrust of these communications was that it was time the schools reviewed their policies and practices in connection with the Christmas season. The feeling here was that sectarian aspects of Christmas did not belong in the public schools. I was sympathetic to that view and appointed a staff committee to explore the whole area of Christmas observance in the schools. This committee was made up of teachers and other certificated staff members, and included a wide range of opinion. After extensive study and discussions, the committee, as might have been expected, crystallized around two positions. The majority favored at least a de-emphasis of the religious aspect of Christmas. A minority, however, felt that the traditional school practices relating to Christmas were both legitimate and desirable. Here is the majority position:

> With regard to religious observances in the public schools, it would be well to keep in mind the religious sensibilities of boys and girls of a variety of faiths. As well, we ought not to allow our schools to become the interpreters of religion to children; this role, in our pluralistic society, ought to be left to religious groups.
>
> As educators, we are bound to give priority to the principle of avoiding violation of any student's individual conscience. We must, therefore, be exceedingly aware of the indirect coercive impact which results from the presentation of religious symbols, songs, decorations, parties, or other materials or scheduled events which do not arise out of an academic study of the nature and role of religion in society. Excusing a child from class, as the Supreme Court has pointed out, does not relieve the inherent compulsion which results from exclusion by one's peers, but rather indicates that the subject matter or the manner or presentation is inappropriate for the pluralistic public school.
>
> It is not the appropriate role of our school system to enter into an area as complex as religious observances and commitment without adequate prior curricular structure. The variety of religious doctrines and interpretations must of necessity be misrepresented in the simplistic treatment which observances and beliefs receive in the present structure.
>
> It should be pointed out that none of the above is to be interpreted as prohibiting brief discussions of Christmas, Pass-

over, Easter, Hanukkah, or other religious subjects when they are initiated by the children themselves as an outgrowth of their daily experiences and study. However, extreme restraint should be exercised in use of any symbols such as the Star of David, crosses, Christmas trees, Hanukkah Menorahs, etc., or songs such as "Jesus Loves Me," "Silent Night," "Away in the Manger," "Presents for Baby Jesus," and "Shima Yisrael," which relate to any specific religion or religious holiday within the school situation unless they are called for specifically by the curriculum, such as courses in comparative religion, or are being used to illustrate the response of one religion to an ethical, philosophical, or social problem being dealt with by the class, as might be necessary in a history lesson.

Units on History of Religions and Cultural Traditions of Americans and World Community Groups, together with the study of Comparative Religions, should be introduced into the school system at the secondary school level as an elective.

Sufficient materials exist in the areas of music, art, and drama to provide for the type of motivated group work which we normally see during the Christmas season, which need not have the detrimental effects of the use of materials which are religiously sectarian in their nature. School librarians and consultants will be able to help provide such materials.

(Signed by eight committee members)

This is the minority statement:

A *religious* holiday observance, as such, is not, I believe, considered in that context when a class gives a Christmas play in the public schools. While the Jewish community may feel that they are discriminated against by the above event, there is really no basis for such bitter feelings. No one religion claims Christmas as its own, therefore, why should one form of belief have such a drastic effect on all other beliefs? Our ancestors came to this land in search of "FREEDOM OF EXPRESSION OF RELIGION." They worked and fought that their descendants would never have to undergo the persecutions they had experienced in the old world. The traditional celebration of the holidays of our country has been passed on as "FREEDOMS" from one generation to another. Does it seem just and

right to deprive little children of the pleasure of these traditions because one group objects to their observance? There is
much "give and take" in the process of living, and it seems
rather ironical that one group would deprive all other groups
of happiness and good will at a season when these feelings are
brought so vividly to our minds and hearts in the songs and
story of Christmas.

The following selection, taken from "The Emerging Elementary Curriculum" by Albert H. Shuster and Milton E.
Ploghoft, is rather interesting in relation to the above subject.
"In the public schools of the United States, moral and ethical
behavior of the type which is stressed by the Judeo-Christian
heritage is an integral aspect of the total classroom environment. Beyond this, appropriate attention should be given to
the role of religion in the history of this nation. Consideration
of the necessity for separation of church and state in a free,
democratic society, the right of religious freedom, and respect
for the religious beliefs of others, are areas that may be properly dealt with in the social studies instruction.

"There is no reason for the school to appear *irreligious* or
anti-religious in its attitudes."

What true American would not resent as an insult the impu-
tation that ours is a godless nation? Houses of Congress open
their proceedings each day with a prayer. The President appoints each year a day of thanksgiving and prayer, and, when
occasion requires it, a day of fasting. Christianity, in fact,
though not legally established, is understood to be the national
religion. No political party is hostile to it, or to any particular
body of Christians. Nearly all the works of active beneficence,
in which no country surpasses the United States, are carried
on by active religious men and women. Our moral standard
is Christian, and religious faith is the paramount impulse to
good. No people has ever become civilized without the guidance of religion, and, if a race of men could be found who
should think there is no God, and that they are the highest
beings in the universe, it is impossible to imagine that they
should not sink to lower and lower planes of life. For such
men, the world could be but a machine, and the enthusiasm
which springs from faith in divine ideals would die within
their hearts. Is this the attitude that we wish to create in the

minds and hearts of our little children by the suppression of anything relating to the Deity in the public schools? I sincerely trust that it is not, and will not be the result of the discussion that is presently taking place regarding Religion (for that is what it really is) in the Berkeley Public Schools.

This being a free country, I feel that if anything should be done regarding the above subject, it should be put to the vote of the people, and let them express their true feelings in a democratic manner at an election.

(Signed by two committee members)

The matter did not end here, however. The PTA explored the topic, as did various staff groups. When I left Berkeley there was growing resistance on the part of individuals and groups within the Christian community to any major de-emphasis of Christmas or other religious holidays in the schools. This issue is far from resolved in Berkeley or elsewhere, and it must be faced by educators.

CLERGYMEN AND RELIGIOUS ORGANIZATIONS

There is as wide a range in relevance and effectiveness in the clergy as in every other profession. In the twenty years I have served as a superintendent, I have found among clergymen those who totally ignore the public schools (and most of the rest of this earthly society as well), those who have a negative influence on education and attempt to restrict the activities of the school to what they consider proper, and those who recognize the schools as partners in the advancement of mankind and who provide genuine support to public education. Fortunately, most clergymen fall in the last bracket.

Members of the clergy are frequent and effective participants in various citizens' committees, sometimes on matters far from their primary expertise. Issues containing moral relevance for society as a whole, such as school desegregation, have found them to be strong supporters. Just before the 1964 recall election in Berkeley—which was held to determine whether or not courageous school board members voting for desegration were to be removed from office—seventy-six community leaders of all major religious faiths signed a statement urging that the board members be sustained and not removed from office. In 1967 and 1968, as Berkeley was moving toward elementary school desegregation, ministers and rabbis were active in our cause. They spoke out publicly in support of integration; they provided forums by having their congregations hear our speakers discuss the issues. Individual churches, church agencies, and councils of churches provided endorsements for the principle of integration.

Clergymen have frequently worked hard to aid the passage of tax elections or budget referendums. Churches have helped the schools by providing needed facilities for programs (early childhood education, adult education) when there has been insufficient space in regular school buildings.

In general I have found that school people and the clergy have a common desire to promote the general uplifting of the community. This makes a ready basis for a genuine partnership. Any school person who is sincerely interested in the betterment of man need have no difficulty in establishing rapport with clergymen of all faiths.

CONCLUSION

Our Constitution and the basic principles on which our pluralistic society was founded require that public schools not become involved in sectarian, devotional exercises and that they refrain from programs whose intent or effect might create a preference for one religion over another. Historically, public schools frequently have violated the principle of separation of Church and State; today, this principle has been more clearly defined and is becoming more commonly accepted.

This does not mean that schools and religion have nothing in common and must remain separated. Schools can teach about religion, about its role in development of various subject areas, about its role in the progress of man through the ages, and about its importance as an institution in society today. However, this must be done in a manner that instills respect for all religions without indicating a preference for a particular one.

If this guideline is followed, organized religion and the schools can play a vital role together in the well-being of an enlightened society. The 138-member Berkeley School Master Plan Committee developed two recommendations regarding the place of religion in the public schools. These recommendations provide a fitting conclusion to this chapter: "It is recommended that observances which tend to emphasize one religious tradition over others be eliminated from the schools," and, "It is recommended that the curriculum include instruction in the historical, sociological, psychological, artistic, and philosophical aspects of the religious dimension of man's experience."

9

The Nonpublic Schools

Share the Load

In early September, 1969, I held a press conference in Berkeley and announced that I was leaving California to become Commissioner of Education in the Commonwealth of Massachusetts. I indicated that my reason for leaving was that I felt the action in education would soon shift from the local level to the state level and that I wanted to be where the action was. I also stated that I considered my new assignment the most challenging and potentially the most difficult in the fifty states.

It was obvious to most educators, by mid 1969, that local school systems were in deep financial trouble. I have pointed out elsewhere in this book that the trouble was caused by the manner in which public schools were financed. We had not sold the need for vast federal and state help to lawmakers in Washington and in our state capitols. As a result we had "broken the back" of the small home owner by increasing the local property tax to levels that were burdensome and, in most cases, excessive. Aware of this, I predicted a collapse of many local school systems, with the state assuming a principal role in the operation of the schools. If this were to happen, I wanted to be at the table where decisions were to be made.

My second point—that I considered the assignment in Massachusetts to be the most challenging and potentially the most difficult—was based on observations I had made on my visits to the Bay State and information that had been given to me by various individuals and groups when they learned that I might be the new commissioner.

One subject alone—the size and financial condition of the parochial school system—was enough to convince me that the position would be challenging. I learned that over 200,000 students attended these schools, and rumors had been widespread that some of these private systems were in serious financial difficulty and faced imminent closing. I knew that I would spend much of my time in the early seventies trying to resolve this intricate legal and educational challenge.

As I reviewed the parochial school problem, I had mixed emotions. I wanted above everything else to have a strong, vibrant public school system. At the same time, I believed in the rights of people to set up nonpublic schools; but by 1969 I had become critical of the "motif" for many of them. It was obvious that in the South private schools were being established so that whites could escape from the public schools (attending school with black children), and it seemed obvious that in many northern cities whites were attempting to enter new private and parochial schools in the suburbs. I did not know how many were running away from the inner city because of the quality of the school program, as compared to the number who refused to accept the integrated school. One thing I did know: blacks were also most unhappy with the quality of the inner-city school and would have fled to the suburb if fair housing practices had made it possible and if they had had the financial means to leave the city.

Another reason for my mixed emotions was my knowledge that thousands of children attending private and parochial schools in this country were receiving a second-class education.

How did I know this? Because I had read the evaluations of these schools made by such distinguished Catholic educators as Father Hesburgh, president of Notre Dame University; because I had visited many of these schools and had spent considerable time reviewing their programs with teachers and administrators; because I have had nieces and nephews come through the system.

Before detailing the shortcomings, let me make it perfectly clear that, like public schools, private and parochial schools are neither all bad nor all good. If they are well financed, they tend to be average or better. If the financial support is not present, they cannot get the job done. It is as simple as that.

What are the major shortcomings of the new private schools in the South and many of the nonpublic schools in the North? They lack adequate staff so necessary to meet the myriad needs of today's student. Counsellors, guidance specialists, and nurses are in short supply. Remedial specialists in reading and speech are rarely available. Classes tend to be excessive in size. Many teachers are not properly prepared. Instructors carry teaching assignments that are excessive. Vocational (occupational) courses tend to be restricted to the business field for women and are almost nonexistent for men. School plants are restrictive in size. Gymnasium and auditorium space is not always available. Textbooks and supplies tend to be in short supply with students required to purchase their own. The supervisory staff is almost nonexistent.

The strength of the nonpublic school in the North was found in the strength of the men and women of the religious orders who gave unselfishly of themselves to make education rewarding to the tens of thousands of young people attending these schools. But now we have a major problem: the number of new teaching vocations in our religious orders has diminished, and laymen, demanding "going salaries" for teachers, must be employed. Thus, the local pastor has a critical money problem: instead of paying a few hundred dollars for a teacher's room and board, he is required to pay salaries in the five to ten thousand dollar range.

The question of support for nonpublic schools is not new. I had been involved in the subject for over twenty years. As a school superintendent in Maine in the late forties and early fifties, I had fought successfully for transporation rights of non-public school students. In the late fifties in New York, I had fought, again successfully, to provide equal health services for nonpublic school students. But, I was anxious to do more: to do what was legally possible and morally and politically correct.

Politically, I needed the support of Catholic parents (sending their children to parochial schools) if the public school budget was to be approved. I felt that wherever possible we should make our public school facilities available to parochial students. In Sanford we built a beautiful new high school gymnasium with a variety of auxiliary rooms. The parochial high school, at that time, had no gymnasium. We shared the facility with them. We also built a new stadium with practice fields; we shared the facility.

I presented a plan to the parochial school people making it possible for their young men to take vocational courses at the public high school, and to take their academic and religious courses in the parochial high school. With students and faculty in the two systems doing the planning, we worked out joint cultural assembly programs. A cooperative health program, with school nurses providing services in both school systems, was implemented. Whenever we changed a reading series or a math series and the material we had been using was in good condition, we offered it to the parochial schools. The same went for equip-ment. When consultants were brought in to work with the pub-lic school staff, we invited the parochial school faculty to join us.

As a result of these efforts, excellent esprit de corps existed between the two systems, and the community solidly supported the public school budget request. (While the public school pros-pered financially, I hasten to point out that the two parochial high schools could not survive—they closed in September, 1969.)

The question of whether direct financial assistance can be given to nonpublic schools will soon be challenged in the Supreme Court of the United States. As we wait for that decision, I feel school administrators—public and nonpublic—should get together at the local level and assess the situation. If the nonpublic school system is well and vibrant—fine. If the system is having trouble, the responsible officials should consider all the alternatives that are or will be legally possible.

On my arrival in Massachusetts, I wanted firsthand information on the magnitude of the problem. I visited the diocese superintendents and asked for their reactions. I met with His Eminence, Richard Cardinal Cushing, on several occasions. Following these meetings, I encouraged His Excellency, Governor Francis Sargent, to move speedily in implementing a General Court decision to have a "Blue" panel named to come to grips with the problem. In addition, I sent the following memorandum to all school people in the Commonwealth.

> Dear Colleague:
>
> At the October meeting of the Board of Education I made the following statement regarding nonpublic schools and how their closing affects local school systems. At this time I would like to share with you my ideas on the subject.
>
> When I first arrived in the Commonwealth, almost nine months ago, I indicated that the first task that I had set for myself was to visit the schools of Massachusetts. Since that time I have sought out those who could give me insight as to where the strengths and weaknesses could be found in this system. I have spoken with superintendents of schools, teachers, principals, school committeemen, legislators, and perhaps the most important of all the representatives of our schools—the children. I have spent considerable time listening to the heads of the state's diocesan schools.
>
> Of particular significance have been the meetings that I have had with His Eminence, Richard Cardinal Cushing. Cardinal Cushing has probably been responsible for the laying of

more cornerstones of educational and medical institutions than any other man in the history of the Church. This great man tells me that he needs help—I do not question that statement. On the contrary, his problem is our problem. Following several weeks of study by personnel within this department on the question of nonpublic schools, I would like to make the following statements:

1. Let it be clearly understood by all that under our present Constitution there can be no direct financial aid to any school not conducted under public auspices.

2. I urge all local school administrators, if they have not done so to date, to establish direct lines of communication with their nonpublic school counterparts to insure that in the event of changes in the latter's plans, the transition of their children to public responsibility will be as smooth as possible.

3. In those cases where such changes appear imminent, I urge that the local public officials examine the possibilities of leasing the schools in question and of employing current staff regardless of their lay or religious status, if it should prove feasible.

4. I urge that legislation be filed to amend the current laws of the Commonwealth that now prevent a community from applying directly to this Department seeking financial assistance in the purchase of an existing school facility that meets State standards. Currently, before a community may apply, special legislation is needed in each individual case. Last year the General Court acted on close to 700 bills relating to education alone. This recommendation is an attempt to reduce that work load.

5. I urge that the Department's budgetary request for fiscal 1971, including funds not only for continued school construction, but also for rehabilitation and renovation, be appropriated. Although the current law was amended in 1968 to include this additional function, funds have never been earmarked for this, nor for the necessary personnel required to follow through on this program. This could be most helpful in the purchase of existing facilities that require modification to meet state standards.

6. I urge that His Excellency, Governor Sargent, move

with all speed to appoint those remaining members of
the Study Commission to examine the whole question
of nonpublic schools. As a member of the Commission,
our report is due in less than fifteen months and we
cannot begin our work until the Governor makes his
appointments.*

As a final note, I urge all local systems to develop a long
range educational plan for their community. Such a plan will
have to take into account all of the children in the area, and
should project future enrollments in both the public and nonpublic systems. I am reminded in this instance of the City of
Brockton, at one time the largest shoe manufacturing city in
the world. Since 1945, Brockton has lost about 80 percent of
her shoe manufacturing facilities, and with this, her population
began to decline. Nevertheless, she put her house in order, and
aggressively recruited industry. Today, Brockton ranks as the
24th fastest growing community in the country on the basis of
population.

Since 1952, $34.5 million has gone into new school construc-
tion. She has either completed or has under construction six
elementary schools and two additions, four junior high
schools, and a high school that will be completed this year that
will be second to none in this nation.

In 1965, it became apparent that the enrollment in the five
parochial elementary schools was beginning to dip. The machinery was set in motion to construct a new 1,000 pupil school
to absorb the anticipated impact that this could have on the
public system. In September of this year, Brockton began
leasing the recently closed St. Coleman's School, and is continuing an analysis of the situation.

It is this type of planning that I applaud, and the people of
Brockton deserve high praise for their efforts.

Sincerely yours,
Neil V. Sullivan
Commissioner of Education

While we wait to see what action the Governor and legislators
will take, other relationships between public and nonpublic

---

*Two days after this request, Governor Sargent made these appoint-
ments.

schools must be understood. Congress, by enacting the Elementary and Secondary Education Act of 1965, opened the door for direct aid to nonpublic school children. Title I, aid to educationally deprived children, directs public school officials to provide equal services for children who fall in this category who attend nonpublic schools. Title II, aid to library resources, directs that instructional material must be on loan to teachers and students in private schools in amounts proportionate to the nonpublic schools. Both programs are now supervised by officials of the State Department of Education (where the action is) and federal guide lines should be vigorously followed so that nonpublic schools will receive fair treatment. On the other hand, nonpublic school administrators must do their share of the necessary homework by carefully documenting what their entitlement is.

One other concept that is receiving considerable attention today is the so-called voucher plan. Under this arrangement a parent would be given an educational voucher for each of his children. The amount of the entitlement would be equal to the per student cost in the local public school system for his education. Where do I stand on this suggestion? I am willing to give it a chance under *carefully* controlled conditions on a pilot basis. Ground rules should be carefully worked out with all members of the educational family participating in any policy decision.

As we move into the seventies, I would like to see several changes in the relationship between nonpublic and public schools. As a Catholic and an educator whose life has been devoted to public school education, I firmly believe that children from all racial, religious, and socioeconomic backgrounds must learn to live together. There is no better way to start than by going to school together and sharing common learning experiences. I do not like to see a student of any race or ethnic or religious group attend a school limited exclusively to members of his own group. In addition to the undesirable feature of isolation, nonpublic schools are running out of money and cannot afford enough good teachers at today's salaries, nor can they buy sufficient technological equipment, to provide top quality education.

For these reasons my position on nonpublic schools differs considerably from that of many of my fellow Catholics. I would like to see parochial schools limit themselves primarily to religion, philosophy, and moral values, and send their students to the public schools for the standard course work in fields such as English, science, mathematics, social studies, the fine arts, physical education, and occupational education. Individual Catholic students could spend a portion of the day in public schools with their peers of differing backgrounds, and part of it in the parochial schools where they could receive the religious training their parents want them to have. This would have the advantage of bringing more Catholic students into contact with non-Catholic students, thereby enriching all of the students. It would also have the effect of freeing parochial schools of the great financial responsibility of the costs of staffing and equipping courses that are *not* primarily religious. (Parochial schools spend approximately 80% of the teaching time on *non*religious activities—a saving to the parish of about 80% could be anticipated.) Parochial schools could concentrate their limited financial resources on those areas in which they are best equipped to offer a unique contribution. Ways and means could be worked out for the joint use of church property for nonreligious instruction (rental is one possibility), and the nonpublic school staff could be given opportunities (for those who need the time) to become fully certified. Such an arrangement would call for close working relationships between the leaders and *staff* and students of the various school systems. This in itself is a worthy objective. Public and parochial schools engaged in such a partnership would reap benefits, and from their association we would have a stronger America.

10

Desegregation

Equality Education

Today the educational leader faces no more crucial question than that of race and education. The spectre of segregation in schools and housing, more than ever, haunts this land. Fourteen years after *Brown* v. *Board of Education,* the overwhelming mass of Negro children in the South still attends predominantly black schools. In the North the picture is even more dismal. Since that 1954 landmark decision, schools in Northern centers of population have become more segregated than ever. Most urban centers are rapidly becoming solid inner-city minority racial ghettos. Public school enrollment in these areas has reflected the population trends around them. The quality of these schools has been allowed to deteriorate. Buildings have been permitted to fall into disrepair. Teachers in too many instances have fled these inner-city schools in favor of service in "better" schools in outlying areas. The deterioration of inner-city schools has increasingly stimulated the desire of remaining Caucasians to flee the area, and so the vicious circle continues.

Although the landmark *Brown* decision promised the legal end of segregation and led to hopes that our society would become more integrated, now, a decade and a half after the decision, the situation is not only worse but is deteriorating rapidly. Not only has the vast bulk of de jure segregation remained intact, but our nation has seen a tremendous growth in de facto segregation—legally different from the de jure segregation of the *Brown* decision, but equally harmful.

Superintendents traditionally have resisted admitting that a problem exists, let alone facing the issue. In times past, to tackle the issue of segregation was to "make waves" that could be avoided if the problem were ignored. The traditional superintendent's party line was to deny any responsibility for racial balance in schools. If the neighborhood school pattern produced racially segregated schools, then this was the fault of segregated housing, and the battle should be fought in that area, not in the area of education. It was the educators' job to provide education for the neighborhood youngsters who showed up at any given school. The fact that in many instances it did not even do this properly is beside the point. My colleagues traditionally have refused to accept the racial composition of individual schools as being their problem.

Now, however, the scene is changing. Educators belatedly are coming to recognize that they cannot escape this issue, and that "not making waves" is no longer a viable alternative. Those waves are going to be made. An increasing number of school administrations across the country are failing because they are not coming up with workable solutions to this problem. Whether or not the educator is compelled to face the issue, there are many legal, academic, psychological, and sociological reasons why he should become interested in desegregation.

LEGAL REASONS

The 1954 decision in *Brown* v. *Board of Education* was based on de jure, not de facto, segregation. However, from the standpoint of the individual child, its conclusion—that segregated

schools are inherently inferior for the minority and majority—
is valid for any kind of segregation. School administrators *must*
be concerned with the harmful effects which segregation im-
poses if they would conform to the spirit of this landmark decision. In many states the courts and other governmental agencies
have gone considerably further than the 1954 decision. Massachusetts, for example, has made satisfactory desegregation a condition for state aid to local districts. That state has gone the furthest
to date in its legal requirements for, and financial support of,
racial balance.

In California, the State Board of Education officially declared
as a matter of policy that "persons or agencies responsible for the
establishment of school attendance centers or the assignment of
pupils thereto shall exert all effort to avoid and eliminate segregation of children on account of race or color." The attorney
general gave an opinion as follows: "The governing board of a
school district may consider race as a factor in adopting a school
attendance plan, if the purpose of considering the racial factor
is to effect desegregation in the schools, and the plan is reasonably related to the accomplishment of that purpose."

The intent of the law is clear. There have been many cases,
with differing results, bearing on the question of *how far* school
officials are compelled to go in combating de facto segregation.
Regardless of how far we are legally forced to go, there are many
reasons why school officials should *want* to take action to improve racial balance.

ACADEMIC REASONS

The bulk of available evidence, although admittedly not exhaustive, tends to support the hypothesis that students drawn
from minority groups or from a lower socioeconomic class
(black or white) achieve more, academically, in schools with
mixed student bodies than they do when segregated. This con-

clusion is supported by studies reported by Havighurst, Wilson, and later by Coleman and his associates in the Office of Education.* This should not be a surprise to anyone who has been exposed to low-income segregated schools. Historically, according to Green,† segregated schools have led to inferior teachers, buildings, textbooks, and equipment—in short, a totally inferior opportunity for minority youngsters. They are, in fact, if not always in theory, the creatures of ghetto economic and social deprivation.

Children are stimulated by contact with those of differing backgrounds. In the case of the disadvantaged minority youngster, such contact frequently results in raising his aspirations. However, the benefit is two-way. The Caucasian child is stimulated and his learning enriched by exposure to the ideas and attitudes of students of different backgrounds. In this day, segregated education spells inferior education for the Caucasian student separated from his community and his world.

PSYCHOLOGICAL REASONS

Crucial to an individual's academic success and his general effectiveness as a citizen is the development of a positive self-image. People must think they are important. Segregation has traditionally carried with it a symbolic rejection by society. In

---

*Robert J. Havighurst, *The Public Schools of Chicago* (Chicago: Board of Education, 1964), pp. 23-51, 57-78, 368-390; Alan B. Wilson, *Educational Consequences of Segregation in a California Community* (Berkeley: University of California Survey Research Center, December 1966), pp. 33-69; James S. Coleman, et al., *Equality of Educational Opportunity*, U.S. Department of Health, Education and Welfare, Office of Education (Washington, D.C.: Government Printing Office, 1966), pp. 20-23, 28-32, 330-334.

†Robert L. Green, et al., *The Educational Status of Children During the First School Year Following Four Years of Little or No Schooling* (East Lansing: Michigan State University, School for Advanced Studies, Research Services, College of Education, 1966), pp. 3-6, 27-45, 104-105.

the case of de jure segregation, this rejection is more than symbolic. It has blocked the South's economic, social, and cultural development, keeping it the semi-feudal captive of the North. The de facto segregated school symbolizes the residential rejection involved in restricting a group to certain neighborhoods. This is true even if educators are not involved in residential discrimination. The fact that the school composition reflects this residential discrimination makes the school symbolic of society's rejection.

The Coleman study stresses the need of the individual student to feel that he has some control over his own destiny. This feeling can hardly be engendered in a school that symbolizes society's rejection of one's race. The psychological effects of the symbol which segregated schools represent make it impossible to accept "separate but equal" schools.

SOCIOLOGICAL REASONS

The mobility of population within our country has helped to create a cultural diversity which is reflected in our communities. If our young people are to be educated for living in this multicultured world, they need contact with other ethnic groups at a very early age. This need applies to all groups—majority as well as minority. Indeed, education of the segregated white child for full participation in today's world is as shoddy as the segregated education provided so many minority children in the ghetto.

Much stereotyping of ethnic groups comes through lack of contact with members of those groups. Racial balance in a school provides opportunity for personal associations to be formed across ethnic lines. Students can learn by actual experience to make their judgments of other people on an individual basis rather than in terms of the group to which they belong. This is important in both directions.

MYTHS CONCERNING INTEGRATION

Once the educator decides that segregation is a problem requiring his attention, and begins to advocate that solutions be sought, he can expect to be barraged with various myths concerning this issue. These myths vary only slightly from community to community.

Myth One: "Segregation is not a problem for educators, but rather a problem of housing patterns and employment discrimination. We professionals must mind our own shop." I hope this myth has been put to bed by the legal, academic, psychological, and sociological cases already made and by the ominous realities of urban and suburban blight.

Myth Two: "Busing for desegregation is inherently wrong." This is absurd. Busing is a-form of transportation and as such is morally neutral. It is not inherently either right or wrong. The purpose and consequences of the busing determine its rightness or wrongness.

The use of buses to transport children to locations where they can achieve a better education is neither new nor rare in this country. Every day over 16,000,000 school children ride approximately 225,000 buses to and from school. Each year these buses will have traveled over 1,800,000,000 miles. (I will let someone else figure out how many round trips to the moon that would be.) The big yellow school bus has become as traditional to American education in the modern era as the little red schoolhouse was in a former period. There are many surveys and reports (including one from the California Highway Patrol) which indicate that the school bus is the safest form of transportation in America.

It is interesting to note that the alleged evils of busing are emphasized only when we are talking about busing for desegregation. When the buses are used in certain sections of the country to transport youngsters past one school to reach another school where the children are of the same race, the hue and cry against busing are not raised. In short, there are those who are perfectly willing to permit busing to be used to maintain segregation but not to end it.

Myth Three: "The education of Caucasian students will suffer because of desegregation." Berkeley's experience indicates that this need not happen. The Coleman Report and the U.S. Civil Rights Commission Report titled *Racial Isolation in the Public Schools* (1967) concur after depth-investigation of the national experience. When desegregation is carefully planned and administered, substantial gains can be made in the achievement of minority youngsters *without* the predicted dire consequences to Caucasian boys and girls.

Myth Four: "Caucasian youngsters will be subjected to increased violence at the hands of minority youngsters." We must face the fact that there always has been some violence among students and that this violence may be increasing, both inside schools and out. In fact, violence appears to be on the increase all around the world, including places with virtually no Negro population. All of us must accept the responsibility for working against student violence—educators, police, parents, lay citizens, and especially the students themselves. However, we should bear in mind that, over the years, the Negro has been on the receiving end of the violence, both physical and moral, more often than the Caucasian. Much of the Negro student's violence is a reaction to traditional white violence, disrespect, and disregard. Administrators in desegregated schools have stated that most "violence" has not had racial overtones.

Again, Berkeley's experience has shown a substantial improvement in the educational environment offered minority youngsters, *without* a corresponding deterioration in the school environment for Caucasians.

Myth Five: "School desegregation will be followed by a mass exodus of Caucasians." Berkeley's experience contradicts this. Our city had a long-standing pattern of gradually declining Caucasian enrollment dating back to the early postwar years, long before any significant action was taken to desegregate. In 1964, after intensive study and discussion by citizens' committees, the school staff, and the community at large, de facto segregation was eliminated at the secondary level. In February 1966, we instituted a "token" busing program as part of our overall Elementary and Secondary Education Act, Title I, program. The student racial censuses, taken over the last two years, have revealed that not only has the steady decline of Caucasian students been stopped, but there has been a slight *increase* in the number of Caucasian students and this percentage of the total student population has stabilized.

It seems especially ironic to me to hear people use the threat of "white exodus" to defend the neighborhood school pattern. This pattern has been manifestly *unsuccessful* in stopping a white exodus in any major school system in the country. In fact, most of the cities that are experiencing dramatic population shifts are on a neighborhood school basis. It seems to me that people who are concerned about the danger of mass white exodus should be willing to try something else.

Desegregation of schools can take place without the dismal consequences predicted in these myths if the action is well planned and executed and if the public is convinced that the quality of schools will not suffer. Actually, with staff commitment and public, political, and financial support, the quality of education for all of the children will vastly improve.

CRITERIA FOR SOLUTIONS

Although cities will vary in their method of attack on the problem and in the details of the solutions they develop, their approaches must meet certain criteria if their solutions are to be genuine.

segregation must in fact be ended. This point should be self-evident. However, in too many cases the so-called solutions developed represent token gestures toward racial balance but do not wipe out de facto segregation. It may not be possible to wipe out de facto segregation totally overnight, but a community must accept the fact that tensions will continue and the problem will not be solved until this result has finally been achieved.

Desegregation must be combined with a general program of educational improvement. It is not enough simply to mix youngsters, many of whom come from a background of educational deprivation. These children must be given special help to overcome this deficit and to succeed in the new environment. Also, large segments of our communities, unconvinced of the educational necessity for integration, must be shown that the new program is in the best interests of all children.

The solution to de facto segregation must involve the *total* community. No area of the city must be made to feel that it is being picked on or sacrificed to solve a total community problem. This means that Negroes cannot be asked to bear the total brunt of the drawbacks (e.g., long distance travel) accompanying desegregation. De facto segregation is a community-wide problem and must be solved on a community-wide basis.

Educators, in working toward the solution to the problems of de facto segregation, must act in good faith and build the confidence of the community in that good faith. Unless such confidence is built securely, educators risk being considered antagonists, and too often are denied the time and community cooperation needed to prepare programs for solving the problems.

PROPOSED SOLUTIONS

Open Enrollment

One of the most common attempts to combat de facto segregation is through some form of open enrollment. Basically, this approach permits students who would normally go to one school to go to another one provided there is room. In general, this plan involves permission for minority students in segregated, low-prestige minority schools to occupy vacancies in higher prestige Caucasian schools in other parts of the city. (Although transfers in the reverse direction are sometimes permitted, it is extremely rare that a significant number of them result.) Usually the transfers are voluntary. Districts having open enrollment vary in their practices concerning transportation of the students: some districts provide it; others leave it as a responsibility of the parents.

Open enrollment, if combined with a program of general educational improvement, can be helpful as a first step in the direction of integration. However, it is totally inadequate as a long-range solution to the problem. There are three basic reasons for this:

The desegregation achieved in the receiving schools is token at best.

The sending schools in almost every case are just as segregated as they were before (and sometimes have been stripped of their leading students). Also, their morale can be adversely affected by the implied criticism of having students leave to seek a "better" situation elsewhere.

A false feeling of accomplishment with having adopted an open enrollment program could get in the way of educators' addressing themselves to the task of developing a genuine solution.

Reverse Busing

This type of program keeps the schools essentially as they are except that they would be desegregated by busing some students at each grade level from segregated Negro schools to segregated Caucasian schools and vice versa. I know of no place in the country where this is being done on any significant scale. To be a genuine desegregating measure this shuttle service would have to encompass almost half of the students in each building involved in the trade. This kind of program differs from the Princeton Plan (which will be discussed later) since both schools continue to serve substantially the same grade levels. Theoretically, complete integration could be achieved by this method. It likewise would fulfill the criterion of involving the total community. However, this kind of program is not realistic in terms of community acceptance. The selection of students at each grade level to be transported to the opposite school poses nearly insurmountable problems. In most communities, two-way busing between Caucasian and minority areas will not provide the answer to de facto segregation. An exception to this is the so-called Princeton Plan, which is discussed next.

Princeton Plan

The Princeton Plan calls for abolishing segregation between two schools by having all of the students of the two combined attendance areas attend one of the schools for certain grades and then all of them go to the other school for other grades. Thus, each of the two schools would draw from the entire combined attendance areas for those grade levels which it serves. The desegregation is total. There have been many modifications of this plan since Princeton, New Jersey, first used it to solve its problems in the late forties. This type of plan, where it can be used feasibly, meets all of the criteria discussed above for a successful solution to de facto segregation. The desegregation is complete; the number of students on each school site at a given grade level is increased, thereby offering greater flexibility in grouping and scheduling and a better chance for teacher specialization and use of specialized equipment. This plan also involves the total community. In a small community like Princeton, with only two schools, such a plan could be effective.

In the large cities this plan is difficult to implement. For prime effectiveness the two schools involved must be close to each other. The segregated Caucasian and segregated Negro schools in the average major city are located far apart, frequently separated by a buffer zone of relatively integrated schools. Thus, finding the schools to match each other in a Princeton Plan would pose difficulties. To be effective in a large city, the plan must be accompanied by a massive two-way busing program. Berkeley, with its four attendance zones, adopted a Princeton-type two-way busing arrangement.

Redistricting

Sometimes it is possible to improve the racial balance between adjacent schools simply by altering the attendance boundary between them. This is rarely satisfactory. First, it is difficult when redrawing boundaries to avoid overloading one school and leaving another with empty space. Second, communities are changing at such a pace that any gains for integration achieved through redistricting are usually short-lived. Third, people affected by the redistricting frequently fight it vehemently. While it is sometimes necessary to move forward with a desirable program in spite of opposition, the relatively minor and temporary gains to be made through redistricting frequently are not worth the antagonism that can be aroused. Redistricting in the big cities also suffers from the same handicap as the Princeton Plan. Only rarely are a segregated Caucasian school and a segregated Negro school side by side. Usually there are intervening schools in various stages of desegregation and transition.

Schools deep in the heart of either a Negro or a Caucasian ghetto are relatively unreachable by this means. Although individual situations might be alleviated in some smaller communities, redistricting is not a promising approach to the problem in the large metropolitan areas.

One-Grade School

This is a modified Princeton approach and has been used in medium-sized cities to overcome de facto segregation among three or more schools at a given level (e.g., elementary, junior high). Berkeley, California, and Teaneck, New Jersey, have used the plan to eliminate segregation at a particular level. Berkeley formerly had three junior high schools, each serving grades seven through nine. This city converted the predominantly Negro junior high school into a school serving all ninth graders in the city. The two remaining junior high schools then divided the city between them for grades seven and eight. Since there were only two schools for grades seven and eight, it was possible to divide the Negro and Caucasian areas of the city between them so that each was a desegregated school. Since Berkeley already had only a single senior high school, this enabled us totally to eliminate de facto segregation at the secondary level. The ninth grade school has been renamed the "West Campus" of Berkeley High School and organizationally is considered to be part of a four-year high school program.

In Teaneck, New Jersey, the concern was at the elementary level. There, a predominantly Negro school was converted into a school serving a single grade, the sixth grade. The remaining schools were made kindergarten through five and the students who formerly would have attended the predominantly Negro elementary school were divided among them. Thus, de facto segregation was wiped out at the elementary level in Teaneck.

As these examples illustrate, the one-grade school can be used in certain situations to achieve integration. The geography of a community and the density of population at each grade level must be considered in this kind of program. These considerations could be limiting factors in very large cities.

Children's Academy

Although it did not provide complete integration, a proposal was developed in Mount Vernon, New York, to provide limited desegregation for each child while retaining use of the neighborhood schools. The Mount Vernon proposal envisioned placing a "Children's Academy" on a large tract of land. All the children in the city would be bused in staggered shifts to this academy for two hours a day. The balance of their program would be spent in their neighborhood schools. The district's various subject area specialists would be assigned to the Children's Academy. Each youngster would have a special program worked out for him at that site. Once the children were bused to the academy, they would be dispersed and would not remain intact as school groups. Thus, for that portion of the day which was spent at the Children's Academy the children would be in a totally desegregated program. Since a third or half of the students would be at the Children's Academy during each period of the day, the neighborhood schools would be accommodating a proportionately smaller group at any given time. This would enable them to make drastic reductions in class size and would provide the opportunity for greater flexibility in grouping and scheduling.

This proposal had the advantage of providing at least some integration for every child in the school system while still making use of the millions of dollars which the district had already invested in its existing school plant. This proposal was attacked, however, from both directions. Those who opposed any integration attacked it as being too great a concession to civil rights groups. The civil rights groups attacked it on the ground that it did not provide *total* integration. The program never really got off the ground.

Educational Parks

There are probably as many definitions for educational parks as there are people defining them. Individual park projects differ in the number of grade levels served, in acreage, in size of attendance area from which students are drawn, and in the type of program envisioned. However, all educational parks have certain features in common. They are designed for a relatively large student population and a large attendance area as compared to the traditional neighborhood school.

By drawing students from many neighborhoods over a large area of the city (or across city lines), educational parks afford greatly improved opportunities for bringing together students of different races, ethnic groups, and social, economic, and cultural strata. In small or medium-sized multi-racial cities such parks can be located to serve all of the children in the community at given grade levels. In larger cities, or communities that are already segregated, these parks can be located near the periphery of the inner city to serve both the minorities of the inner city and the Caucasian students living nearer the city limits and in suburban areas. It is important in locating an educational park that it be readily accessible to all racial groups. Although the local topography will affect decisions about where parks are located, these parks should be placed so that no single racial group feels that it must bear an unfair share of transportation problems.

Educational parks are justifiable also from the standpoint of other important educational considerations. The large number of students at each grade level greatly enhances the possibilities for flexible scheduling and for large and small group instruction, thus increasing the number of electives that can be offered feasibly. This concentration of students also permits more economical use of highly specialized, expensive equipment. Staff specialists can be more effectively utilized since they need not spend time traveling from school to school. More effective and economical use can be made of expensive facilities (such as gymnasiums, libraries, cafeterias, and auditoriums) by eliminating the need for duplication in small neighborhood schools all over the district.

The educational park concept is promising both as an avenue of attack on de facto segregation and as a means of making significant improvements in our educational programs.

The above discussion outlines major types of program that have been developed in an effort to come to grips with the de facto segregation problem. There are probably as many variations of these ideas as there are communities that have tried them. In many instances satisfactory local programs have been developed along the lines of one or a combination of some of the plans I have discussed. Each community must develop its own solution to the problem and must consider local needs and circumstances. Approaches to the problem may vary from place to place, but all communities have one thing in common—they must use *some* approach. They can no longer evade this issue!

II

Integration

Toward a More Perfect Union

Frequently the terms *desegregation* and *integration* are used interchangeably to denote the opposite of segregation. As long as the exact meaning is clearly delineated, I have no objection to either term. However, the words *desegregation* and *integration* are not synonymous. Rather, they are complementary stages in the development of positive race relations. When I use the word *desegregation*, I mean the achievement of racial balance among the schools of a given district—the process of breaking down segregation, de facto or de jure. The word *integration* goes further. It refers to the development of positive relationships and attitudes across racial and ethnic lines and the general acceptance of people as human beings, whoever they are, whatever their backgrounds or beliefs.

Integration builds upon desegregation. Before integration can occur, schools must be desegregated. Desegregation is a crucial step and represents a tremendous victory when achieved, but it is not the whole battle. Once desegregation has been accomplished, integration, the greater achievement, must follow. This is not a simple task. I could cite countless examples of individual schools that are racially well balanced but not successfully integrated. Their students, therefore, are not yet prepared for life in a multi-racial world.

Some of the educational factors that need to be reexamined and redefined, if the goal of integration is to be reached, include staff, curriculum, and organization of students.

THE STAFF

I say flatly that integration will not take place in any school, whatever the racial composition of the student population, unless the teachers take a positive and active role in achieving it. Teachers who do not believe in integration will consciously or subconsciously defeat efforts to bring it about. I have known all too many teachers basically racist at heart who are confused by the terms *desegregation* and *integration,* and determined to keep both from working. They have frequently succeeded—at least for a time. I have known other teachers who did not oppose integration overtly, but did so passively (and Gandhi himself could have learned passive resistance techniques from them!). The teacher who does not believe in integration, who does not want it to work, clearly has no place on the faculty of a racially balanced school—or any other school, in my opinion.

The greater danger is not from teachers who openly oppose integration. In fact, it is the rare teacher who will openly declare his opposition in a school district that has moved to desegregate its schools. A more serious threat is posed by teachers, well-meaning or not, who simply do not understand the problem. Teachers who are subject-matter oriented and who proceed on a business-as-usual basis can undermine integration efforts just as effectively as if that were their intent. How, then, are school faculties to be trained, encouraged, and developed to make integration possible?

In the first place the faculty itself must be integrated and should reflect as fairly as possible the various ethnic groups in the community. The staff members, in addition to being competent, must be able to relate well to students, to respect them as individuals, and to command their respect. Young people from every walk of life (especially those who have had no one to look up to or to identify with) need contact with individuals who, despite wide diversity in racial, ethnic, and economic backgrounds, have "made it" in prestigious occupations—and teaching is one such respected and important occupation. Observing a group of teachers working together in harmony, respecting one another's differences, and moving toward a common goal of integration, will accomplish infinitely more than laying down rules and making demands will accomplish.

It is crucial, then, for any district that wants to integrate its schools to gather an interracial staff. It is not enough to eliminate existing discrimination in employment. It is not enough to let it be known that members of all races will be considered on their merits. School districts must actively seek out applicants from minority groups that have heretofore been denied equal opportunity. It may be difficult for school districts to find enough black recruits immediately. This is the price we are paying for the decades when black youngsters were discouraged from entering any profession requiring higher education. Discriminatory practices, which effectively counseled most black young people out of professional training programs, have created the current shortage of black men and women prepared to be teachers. In one recent year fewer than thirty new black teachers were sent into the profession from all of the combined teacher training institutions in the state of California. This shortage of black teachers provides a ready-made excuse for school districts that wish to avoid employing them. However, for the school district that wants to integrate its faculties, the local shortage becomes an extra challenge.

In Berkeley, hundreds more applicants apply than can possibly be placed. But we discovered that too few were from minority groups and that, if racial balance of the school faculties was to be achieved, there had to be an aggressive recruiting of applicants from minority backgrounds. Teams of staff members under the leadership of the Personnel Department were sent into the South as well as the cities of the North, primarily to recruit qualified teachers for Berkeley. But these teams had another purpose as well. As they moved from college campus to college campus, they sought opportunities to speak to student gatherings and to convey the message that a major school system not only was willing but was actively seeking to employ members of minority backgrounds. In addition, the teams attempted to stimulate interest in education as a career, whether the students wanted to come to Berkeley or not. It is up to educators to stimulate and encourage young people of minority groups to enter the field of education as career teachers, administrators, and leaders, if the talent pool is to grow to serve the needs of all school districts that are trying seriously to integrate their schools. There can be no let-up until all school districts have fulfilled this obligation.

Berkeley recruiting teams were interested to note the competition for promising black students, not only by "newly enlightened" school districts, but by business and industry as well. It is a simple fact of life today that more barriers against minority employment are dropping than there are people qualified to take advantage of the new opportunities. This places a premium on those young people who are adequately prepared, and makes mandatory a national crash program to make up for the years of neglect and to develop a manpower pool of minority group members in the professional ranks.

Through these recruiting teams and through the reputation achieved nationally in the realm of civil rights, Berkeley has been more successful than most districts in obtaining a substantial number of Negro applicants. However, in terms of the percentage of minority group members on our school staff, the pace has not been rapid enough. While plans were being developed for the total desegregation of our elementary schools, representatives of a variety of black organizations and causes in the city visited me. These citizens were willing to support student desegregation, but also made it clear that they felt the employment of black staff members was an essential ingredient of the program. I concurred. So did the Board of Education, and it formally adopted the following statement of policy:

> It is the policy of this Board of Education to implement integration of the District's staff so that the benefits of integration will be readily apparent to all students throughout all categories of employment.
>
> Further, we believe that implementation should move toward a more proportionate staff representation of the racial composition of the student body and community.
>
> Therefore, appropriate and immediate efforts shall be made by the administration to accomplish this goal by the employment of qualified staff for position vacancies.
>
> The administration is hereby instructed to present an annual report on progress in implementing the above-mentioned goal.

The policy statement, while stopping short of a commitment to a rigid quota system, nevertheless set the school district firmly on record as encouraging the employment of qualified members of all racial groups. It further committed the district to sincere efforts actively to seek out minority applicants. The goal was to move toward staff proportions that more nearly corresponded to the racial makeup of the student body. Although not given a year by year quota, the administration was instructed to come in with an annual report on our efforts and our success in fulfilling this policy. More school districts are going to have to make this kind of policy commitment if they are to obtain minority teachers and successfully to integrate their school faculties.

The employment of minority teachers, however, is only part of the task. They must then be deployed in such a way that each school faculty receives maximum benefit. Too frequently school systems have a better record on employing minority teachers than they do on their placement. The tendency has been to place minority teachers in schools with minority students. I have been told that Berkeley, prior to my coming there, tended to follow this pattern. Besides robbing Caucasian youngsters of the opportunity of working with black teachers, it weakens the impact of integrated staffs working together and the example which such cooperation sets for students. Effective integration, then, requires not only that minority teachers be actively recruited, but also that they be deployed so that students and teachers in all schools are brought into close contact with them. Without an integrated school staff, integration cannot succeed.

Intergroup Education

To achieve total and meaningful integration, employment of minority teachers and their effective deployment throughout the entire school system are vital. But racial balance alone is not enough. Teacher training programs in most of our colleges and universities have been noticeably lacking in intergroup education. Teacher training has concentrated too intensively on subject matter and teaching techniques. Important as these are, they are not adequate for today's interracial schools. Teachers must be taught to understand the backgrounds and problems of their students. With such training hopefully will come empathy and skills in promoting integration.

The more forward-looking teacher training institutions are beginning to add this dimension to their programs. Too many schools of education, however, are still ignoring it or are doing only a superficial job. No school district can assume that the teachers it hires will come to the district adequately prepared to further integration. The school district that wants to integrate its schools will have to provide an effective intergroup education program of its own for its staff members. Such in-service training should include the history and culture of various minority groups, and problems that are unique to each minority. Teachers need to be sensitized to life as seen through the eyes of people with different ethnic backgrounds. They need also to come to grips with their own deep-seated and perhaps unrecognized racism, which might prevent their being effective with people from other backgrounds. I believe in the capacity of most human beings to confront their own prejudices and rid themselves of this deterrent to their own growth and development. It is far preferable to help a teacher gain the necessary insights and understanding than to dismiss him because he cannot relate effectively with people of different backgrounds.

In my experience, most teachers, who take seriously their obligation to *all* students, welcome the kind of in-service training that will help them to achieve this goal. In Berkeley, both teacher organizations supported the board of education when it mandated a program of in-service training in minority history and culture. In-service training does add an extra load, but teachers do not oppose it when it is designed to meet a recognized need. In-service training should be given during school time, or teachers should be paid for the time they give—either in dollars or in unit credits on the salary schedule, on the same basis as for units taken at a university.

THE CURRICULUM

Until very recently the curriculum of the typical school systematically excluded minority groups from any meaningful recognition. The United States history courses made it appear that the only people who counted in the development of this country were those whose ancestors came from northern Europe. Primary readers featured blond and blue-eyed youngsters Dick and Jane, with their nice, clean dog, Spot, curled up before the cozy suburban fireplace or prancing on the well-tended suburban lawn. Where Negroes were mentioned at all, it was generally in an abbreviated mention of slavery, or they were portrayed in some menial capacity. About the only favorable reference to the black race was in some grudging recognition of Booker T. Washington or George Washington Carver. Even references to slavery glossed over its horrors and made the slaves seem fairly simple-minded, musical, light-hearted, and protected by their owners. Omitted from the typical history textbook was any reference to Frederick Douglas, Nat Turner, or others in the heroic struggle for emancipation. Omitted, too, was the recognition of the invaluable contribution to the development of America made by countless black citizens, slave and free, since the earliest days of our history.

The typical Dick and Jane readers may contain words designed to stimulate reading skill, but their picture of life relates to only a small segment of America. Is it any wonder that children from minority backgrounds fail to identify with the material and find it totally lacking in relevance and interest? Most of our reading programs make the assumption that the child is from a middle-class background. Such programs are oblivious to the surroundings and conditions which many youngsters bring to kindergarten and first grade. A child who has had little exposure to the English language, to books or other cultural advantages, can hardly be expected to progress in a program designed for a child who comes from an academically stimulating environment or one in which English is always used.

During the early and mid-sixties, some of the more enterprising school systems in America began taking note of this lack in the materials used in our elementary reading programs. The first few efforts at correction were somewhat ludicrous (for example, subtly painting some of the faces black but leaving the rest of the environment intact). However, the need to present more realistic subject matter in the reading programs is at last being recognized and publishers are beginning to provide some improved material.

Black people are not the only minority group which has been

slighted in the curriculum. History has been consistently unfair to the American Indian as well. Most of our children know the Indian as the enemy who burned settlements, scalped his victims, and stood in the way of the development of America. The fact that the Indian was systematically robbed of his land and cruelly restricted by society as a whole is conveniently overlooked. So is the abject poverty under which many Indians live today.

Mexican-Americans have fared little better. Treatment of Orientals (for example, recognition of the Chinese-Americans in building the transcontinental railroad, abuse of Japanese-Americans during World War II) is likewise totally inadequate. And yet members of all these racial groups have not only made significant contributions to the evolution of America, but all of them together *are* America. If they are to function effectively as citizens, however, they are going to have to be made to feel a part of this country, full citizens, respected as individual human beings and members of society. This will not happen if our curriculum remains limited and one-sided. The curriculum must delineate clearly the fact that every human being is important and that society is made up of a large number of ethnic groups that are equal in value.

"Compensatory" Education

Compensatory education, in too many instances, has been used as a substitute for desegregation, not as a part of integration. Most communities with segregated schools, whether de facto or de jure, have a history of neglecting those schools catering primarily to minority students. When this neglect led to a drive for desegregation, a great clamor arose for "compensatory" education to overcome some of the effects of society's neglect of minority youngsters. The general idea was to compensate, not integrate, by giving extra services in predominantly minority schools. These services included lower class size, added specialist service, and improved equipment. The motivation behind many drives for compensatory education was to remove the pressure for school desegregation.

No effective educator can fail to recognize that school desegregation and integration are absolutely necessary in a multi-racial society. But we cannot simply put the kids together and expect miracles. The years of neglect of the minority students will not simply disappear. Extra efforts must be made to help educationally deprived students to succeed. Many services included in a typical compensatory education program are still needed in a program of desegregation, but they are not to be used as a substitute for desegregation. Hopefully, the need for special compensatory education for minority groups will disappear as their educational deprivation disappears.

Tracking and Ability Grouping

A formidable block to the integration of any school, whatever its racial balance, is a rigid system of tracking and ability grouping. Tracking is the assignment of a youngster to a given track, generally based on achievement and so-called I.Q. tests taken at an early age. Such assignment too often restricts a child's options as he grows to adulthood. Thus, early in their educational careers some youngsters are put on a "blue-collar" track that limits them to blue-collar employment upon graduation from high school. Other students are put in a track that prepares them for Ivy League colleges or a variety of other alternatives. I categorically reject such tracking, particularly when it is based upon such faulty criteria as standardized test scores.

Ability grouping has been used as synonymous with tracking, although in most places it refers to a division or grouping within a given subject area (such as English or science). Ability grouping is not quite so rigid as tracking, but both have had the effect of creating segregation within interracial high schools, and have presented major hurdles in the development of meaningful integration.

Flexible grouping, used as a temporary measure for particular students, is acceptable for a limited time. But any grouping that has the effect of closing options to certain youngsters, or gets in the way of achieving integration within interracial schools, is totally unacceptable. Most of the claims for the academic necessity of grouping are either invalid or presuppose the continued inability of teachers to individualize their instruction. In most subject areas students will learn when effectively taught, regardless of the range of ability levels of their classmates. In fact, in some subject areas (for example, social studies) the wider the range of opinion the greater the learning possible in classroom discussions.

Classroom organization does vary, but the goal should not; it should be maximum heterogeneity consistent with excellent academic achievement. The burden of proof must be borne by any variation from heterogeneous grouping. Furthermore, such variation must be flexible and must aim toward the achievement of student integration as well as quality education.

Integration is a far more complex and illusive goal than is desegregation. However, it is a goal which we must continue to pursue after our schools have been desegregated. Integration requires adequate numbers of teachers of various ethnic groups. The integrated staff, to be effective, must understand the history and culture of the various minority groups represented in the school. Curriculum must be stimulating and relevant to each student. Students who need special help and attention must receive it. Grouping practices must be carefully scrutinized and altered when they are found to be interfering with the achievement of integration. Today's educator must never forget that desegregation is only part of the goal in the important task of ending racial imbalance. The ultimate goal is quality education for each child in accordance with his own special needs and abilities.

12

Extremism

No-Man's-Land

If I had any thought that by leaving Prince Edward County for "liberal" Berkeley I was escaping encounters with extremists, I was soon disabused of that notion. I found, upon my arrival in the Athens of the West, a city torn with dissension over the integration of the junior high schools. Members of the Board of Education who had voted to desegregate the schools were having to fight removal from the school board for their courageous action. The recall election was scheduled for October 6, 1964, just five weeks after I assumed office as Berkeley's new Superintendent of Schools. Of course, not everyone associated with the recall election could be called an extremist. However, the climate created by this recall campaign permitted extremists and extremism to have a field day. Rumors, unsigned letters, and vicious verbal assaults were rampant during this period. One member of our staff, whose daughter would be attending the newly desegregated ninth-grade school, was told: "I hope your daughter is the first one raped."

Fortunately the recall was defeated decisively. The courageous school board members who had been willing to risk their political positions for a moral issue were vindicated. Although this was a trying period for the board members and their supporters, in retrospect it was an excellent experience for Berkeley. It demonstrated that school board members could make courageous decisions and still remain in office.

Not many months later our schools were visited by citizens who wanted to check our libraries to see if we were stocking proscribed books or books by proscribed authors. They were particularly interested in works by Langston Hughes, but they did not stop there. Other authors on the list included Pearl Buck, Eleanor Roosevelt, and Carl Sandburg. Although disclaiming any interest in book burning or taking books off shelves, they expressed a desire to have pro-American and "pro-democracy" books included. They were also concerned that one of the music textbooks did not include enough "patriotic" songs. Similar visits were being made by "patriots" in surrounding districts.

In addition to visiting several of our school libraries, a delegation came to see me. I made it clear to them that I was not going to play censor, nor was I going to embark on any book-burning campaign. I had full confidence in my professional staff and would rely on their judgment regarding appropriate material for use in our instructional program and for stocking on our library shelves. A formal presentation was made later to our school board and met the same response. Berkeley's board members demonstrated again that they were not to be stampeded.

This series of incidents led to the one and only direct personal contact that I had with our State Superintendent of Public Instruction, Dr. Max Rafferty. He called to inform me that a delegation from Berkeley had visited him, and he invited me to come to Sacramento to discuss the situation. I accepted. When I arrived, the question of library books became a relatively minor part of the visit. He reviewed briefly the complaints of his visitors concerning our library books and turned the problem back to me, where it belonged. Our discussion then turned to the wider scope of education, including Berkeley's progress in integration. I felt he acted in a most ethical manner, both as an educator and as a man. He had no choice but to listen to complaints from Berkeley. He followed the ethically correct procedure of getting in touch with the local superintendent and turning the problem back over to him. He was also courteous and invited me to have one of my staff members write an article describing Berkeley's junior high school desegregation plan for the monthly magazine put out by the State Department of Education. Throughout this particular episode, I felt his relations with me on that occasion, both professionally and personally, were above reproach.

After the refusal of the school board and the local superintendent to be stampeded and the failure of the State Superintendent to become involved, the assault on our libraries faded away. However, there was more to come. As the honeymoon ended, and as it became increasingly apparent that I was an implacable foe of segregation, the personal assaults began—not all of them from Berkeley. These assaults ranged from reasoned statements of disagreement to anonymous communications of unbelievable viciousness. Many were totally irrational. Several contained an element of threat to me, personally and professionally.

My own inclination was to consign such epistles to the round file immediately. My assistant (who is collaborating on this book) prevailed upon me to turn them over to him to be filed for possible future use in writings or speeches. The grammar, punctuation, capitalization, and wording in these communications speak for themselves. Here are a few examples:

> What a do-gooder you are Sooner than you think you yourself will be running for cover Like other planners. your day is close at hand.
> With a name like Sullivan you must be negroid. Status building you know. If white you are beneath contempt. Berkeley is doomed. At least for what it is worth you are one of its

architects of its destruction. But Mr. Black implement the plan
and youll run like a scared hare Yours in total disgust.

Here is another one that is addressed to the school board.
Unlike most of the letters, this one at least was signed by a
perennial candidate of the right-wing forces.

> Congratulations of your perfect integration—and may all
> your grandchildren be Ubangis. The Caucasian race is not
> worth saving anyway.
>
> I just received your latest propaganda sheet concerning the
> new school term.
>
> All I can say is that you are so screwed up, it's pitiful.
>
> You are the biggest foul ball ever to hit the field of educa-
> tion. Your whole integration hoax is based on error and con-
> trary to all laws of evidence provided by nature—as well as
> contrary to non-pseudo anthropology.
>
> We don't need any carpet bagger pedagogic hacks around
> here. Why don't you pack up and leave.

This one was headed "Christmas, 1968, With other Berkeley
parents I hope that you had a much deserved miserable Christmas and will have a disastrous New Year, as a reward for what
you have done to us and to our children."

> Too bad you have not joined those other too-articulate sabo-
> teurs, MLK, JFK, Joe Lohman and Norman Thomas who left
> us in 1968. I have been vainly hoping that someone would put
> a shotgun up against you and pull the trigger. Couldn't you
> jump off one of the bridges before January 1? It is important
> that you should not carry your infection back to Massachu-
> setts.
>
> Perhaps some day you will recognize the crimes you have
> committed in the name of demorcracy and for the cause of
> socialism. At least you already know how much you are de-
> tested and that the very people you pretend to help have
> rejected the dogma under which you operate. Like the hippes
> you intend to destroy what others built because you set your
> objectives above those of the taxpayers who at the moment are
> paying for your mistakes.

> At least we are fortunate to be rid of you, though your pernicious influence will bring us grief, destruction, hatred and distrust for many years to come. Bad cess to you forever!

My wife and I also received innumerable phone calls, ranging from short, succinct threats to long, haranguing diatribes. Although our phone was unlisted, some of these callers did get through. Eventually we simply hung up the minute a call became threatening or the caller refused to identify himself. Communications of this type were to become a fact of life for the rest of my stay in Berkeley.

In view of the ugliness of the national mood during the summer of 1968 following the assassinations of Martin Luther King, Jr. and Robert F. Kennedy, members of my staff expressed concern for my physical safety and urged me to avoid being alone in situations where I would be physically vulnerable. I appreciated their concern but refused to alter my normal life pattern. Fortunately, extremists in this area were content with phone calls or written messages of hate and did not express their hostility in physical terms.

I am sure that this type of experience is not unique to me. All across the country, superintendents who have sincerely attempted to come to grips with major social and educational issues could recount similar experiences. During the time I was in Berkeley, a superintendent in another Bay Area district became embroiled in a bitter hassle with the president of his school board over the use of the film *Nothing But a Man* in the high school. This film presents a sensitive and dramatic account of racial injustice and the plight of the Southern Negro. The school board president, a conservative Protestant minister, objected to the film on the grounds of alleged obscenity. One of the scenes in the film showed a married couple getting into bed and turning out the lights. He got hung up on this scene and overlooked the central message of the film as well as its educational value in depicting conditions faced by a persecuted minority. The superintendent stood his ground and his opinion was sustained. In fact, the school board president was recalled from office a short time later. During this episode I not only assured this superintendent of my personal support, but made that support public in one of my weekly columns in the local Berkeley newspaper. True, that picture depicted "obscenity," but it had nothing to do with any sexy scenes. The obscenity presented in that film is the inhumanity of man to man. The obscenity is in the condition, not in the film. If we are ever to eradicate this obscenity, it won't be by shielding our young people from the truth concerning it.

In another Bay Area district the superintendent was also subjected to verbal assault and threats because he, too, decided to move forward with integration. He and his wife received phone calls warning him to take a different route to work each day. (This reminds me of what one philosophy professor used to say: "The telephone is an unfortunate invention. Any fool can call you up, and you never know until you answer the phone whether or not he has!")

One of the crowning touches in my own encounter with extremists in Berkeley was a rumor campaign which was mounted late in my administration during the period in which we were moving toward elementary desegregation. One of my assistants (co-author of this book) brought me word of an encounter between another staff member and a lady in the community. This lady told our staff member that she opposed the direction in which we were moving and would fight tooth and nail against things we were trying to accomplish. However, she wanted us to know that she could not countenance what some of her colleagues were about to do. She said that many of her confederates were going to attempt to plant a scandal about me; they had tried by every other means to stop me and had failed, and this was a last resort. She wanted the staff member to know that she would personally have nothing to do with this and that she did not condone it. While she was opposed to us, her opposition would be open and aboveboard. The staff member involved promptly brought that news to my assistant, who, of course, relayed it to me.

In too many cases a group, desperate enough and trying hard enough, can succeed in besmirching a public official with the appearance of scandal, regardless of his personal and professional integrity and honor. Fortunately in this instance, although strong effort was made to spread rumors, they did not "take." This kind of campaign represented an unusually vicious and unpleasant form of harassment, but it did not hurt me professionally nor did it interfere with the operation of the schools or the orderly progress toward desegregation.

Any superintendent today who sees his role as encompassing more than simply managing schools and who recognizes his responsibility as a leader in helping the school district and the community to focus on major educational and social issues must be prepared to contend with the extremists in his community. Many of these extremists will be crackpots who need not be taken seriously—except for taking care to negate any mischief they might cause. Other extremists arrive at their positions through sincere but misguided motives often caused by fear. Many insecure people are afraid to face the fact that social changes must occur, and tend to view with suspicion anyone who attempts to bring about such changes.

Today's educator, if he takes seriously his leadership responsibility, must be sufficiently secure inwardly to be able to stand confidently against those who would purge libraries, teach hate, or convey personal threats. Having the hide of a rhinoceros helps to keep him impervious to this kind of assault. Harry Truman's admonition applies today as well—not only to government but to educational leadership: "If you can't stand the heat, stay out of the kitchen."

13

The Rise of Militancy

A Piece of the Action

A presidential candidate is faced with hecklers almost everywhere he goes. Another candidate cuts short a speech when he
is drowned out by protesters. A liberal college president, under
fire for his restraint in dealing with student activists, later finds
his position made untenable by those very activists. Burning of
draft cards, anti-war demonstrations, and sit-ins at induction centers are a regular occurrence. Black citizens appear before governing bodies and public officials to demand rights that are theirs
by birth. The list could go on and on.

Never, outside of a period of civil war, have the basic ground
rules of American society been so severely challenged. People
who have been substantially prevented from influencing decisions which affect them, and who have been far removed from
sources of power, are demanding change—and they are not
being polite about it! In some instances this rising militancy has
led to desirable reforms. In other instances it has merely stiff-
ened the backs of those who oppose significant change. Various
factions chant the slogans: "Freedom Now," "Law and Order,"
"Hell, No, We Won't Go!" To some the only solution is the total
overthrow of society or of the particular institution under attack.

To others the only answer to the militant demands for change is a rigid suppression by force. Most Americans stand somewhere between these extremes.

The current wave of militancy and of vigorously asserted dissent differs from earlier history mainly in degree rather than in kind. Super-patriots to the contrary, our history teaches us that there is nothing "un-American" about citizens expressing their displeasure in a militant manner. Although I certainly do not condone or advocate all of the tactics that have been utilized in the name of dissent, we do not have to look hard to find plenty of precedents in our history. Sometimes militant and even violent protest has been successful. Other times, it has not. In some instances the instigators are now America's venerated heroes, and the acts themselves are pointed to with pride by even the most rabid patriots. Let us take a look at examples of militancy in American history.

MILITANCY: EARLY AMERICAN STYLE

Our colonial history is full of examples of individuals and groups refusing to accept a given situation or to act in a certain manner decreed by duly constituted authorities. In fact, many of the earliest Americans were here precisely because their dissent created problems for them with someone on the other side of the ocean. The early American Quakers, for example, had been persecuted in England because of their refusal to participate in war. They even caused trouble because they would not remove their hats in front of high officials. (How would that kind of requirement grab our younger generation!) In early New England the colonists simply drove out the governor of the short-lived and hated dominion after King James II was overthrown.

The period between the close of the French and Indian War and the outbreak of the Revolutionary War is full of examples of forceful dissent from unpopular government decree. After the hated Stamp Act had been passed by Parliament, it was not "friendly persuasion" that prevented stamps from being landed in many ports, or that discouraged distributors of the stamps from functioning. The Sons of Liberty was *not* an organization that restricted itself to discussing rationally the pros and cons of the various pieces of parliamentary legislation then affecting the colonies. In that period, as well as this, the boycott was used to exert pressure. The boycott of British goods at that time led British merchants to put pressure on Parliament to be more reasonable.

The classic example was the Boston Tea Party. Not only was there illegal forced entry onto ships, but there was also considerable destruction of private property in support of a principle regarding taxation. Aside from the destruction of property, however, from the British view the Tea Party represented the ultimate impudence to duly constituted authority. I am not sure that the words "law and order" were used then, but the authorities were clearly not amused. Their response to the City of Boston would do credit to the most vocal stiflers of dissent today. And yet American history, in spite of the illegality of these incidents and the destruction of property involved, clearly identifies with the activists, rather than the side of "law and order."

A few years later, after the winning of independence, in western Massachusetts a group of veterans, with honorable service records in the Revolutionary War, organized under Daniel Shays in an effort to prevent what was to them burdensome taxation to repay the state's war debt to wealthy citizens. This incident was called Shays's Rebellion. It took the State Militia to put it down.

Even George Washington had his troubles with the Whiskey Rebellion of 1794. The farmers of western Pennsylvania took matters into their own hands when they felt that the Federal tax on whiskey placed an unfair and severe burden upon them. This whiskey tax was enforced only when the President called out the troops and sent them to quell the "rebellion."

Today's protests at induction centers pale in comparison to the draft riots of July 1863, during a period in which America was literally fighting for its life. If there ever were made-to-order moral issues that could be used in "selling" a war, the preservation of the Union and the freeing of human beings from slavery would certainly be powerful ones. However, in spite of the justice of the cause, the draft was greeted by four days of mob violence in New York City.

These cases present examples in which citizens reacted militantly when they felt their rights were not being respected or when some other moral issue was involved. Thus, although today's rise of militancy is much more widespread, much more varied in terms of people involved and the issues and the tactics employed than would have been true at any other period, our study of history shows that today's activists have plenty of precedents. Thus, militancy per se is not an un-American phenomenon, although the tactics employed in any given situation might be inconsistent with a democratic society.

Our history indicates that militant activity frequently led to changes in society itself, whether or not the changes were precisely those originally sought by the militants. The militancy of the colonists ultimately led to the independence of this country. The militancy of the abolitionists ultimately led to a war that destroyed slavery, and at the same time confirmed the indivisibility of the nation.

Militancy is inevitable in any democratic society whose citizenry is educated and informed. If citizens are educated, they will think for themselves. If they are informed, they will recognize the imperfections of even the best society. And if the society is a democratic one, its citizens will be accustomed to articulating that dissatisfaction in attempting to remedy the causes of it. The fact that this occasionally leads to a situation that gets out of hand does not detract from the fact that militancy is here and is not going to be shut off as long as our society remains basically democratic.

MILITANCY: A CHALLENGE FOR THE EDUCATOR

Why this discourse on militancy in a book about the changing role of the educator? Why is this a problem for the educators?

In the first place, the schools cannot be totally divorced from their setting. Occurrences outside the school have a definite impact upon the lives of people involved in school and on the activities in the school itself. Public information media are too numerous to permit schools to remain isolated from events in the community surrounding them.

In the second place, and more directly relevant, schools are experiencing the same kind of militancy that is being exhibited in the society at large. This militancy is emerging in each of the three major constituencies of the educator: the students, the staff, and the community. The effectiveness—in fact the survival—of the educator in the years ahead will depend increasingly on his ability to rise to the challenges he will face in each of these constituencies. A failure in any one is sufficient to mar his effectiveness seriously, and even, perhaps, to bring down his administration.

Student Militancy

In the popular fancy of an earlier era, "school days" meant the three Rs and the hickory stick. Youngsters were in school to receive what the teacher had to give them. The model student attended school regularly and on time, turned in his homework, and was very polite to his superior, the teacher. The teacher had a body of knowledge and a set of skills to impart to the youngsters. The students had virtually nothing to say about what they wanted to learn, nor did the teacher. The content in the various subject matter fields was considered its own justification regardless of its relevance for the individual student. The curriculum was content-oriented, rather than student-oriented. The presentation was teacher-oriented, rather than student-oriented. The student was simply the receptacle, the teacher the agent, and the subject content the focal point.

Under that kind of system, the teacher felt it necessary to maintain absolute control of the class. A teacher's effectiveness was often measured in large part by whether or not he maintained good discipline. If there was any evaluation at all concerning a teacher's success in actually teaching anything to the youngsters, it generally centered around their comparative scores on state-sponsored standardized tests.

The rank and file of teachers were undoubtedly good people who sincerely wanted their students to succeed. However, teaching was such a narrowly prescribed function, and the curriculum was so unimaginative, that little creativity or meaningful interaction with students was stimulated. There were occasionally teachers who, because of their own strength, managed to pack a wallop in spite of the system, but they were a decided minority.

The movie *Good Morning, Miss Dove*, produced only about a decade ago, portrayed an image of the teacher in terms of strict discipline and preparation for the state tests. Although Miss Dove emerges in the movie as highly respected by her former students, teachers in that image will not be adequate to face the challenges posed by rising student militancy. It is not my intent in this book to debunk the respect earned by good teachers of the past. However, my experience as a superintendent, particularly in recent years, compels me to state categorically that the days of the narrow, content-centered curriculum taught by authoritarian teachers (however benevolent) to docile and uncritical students have almost disappeared.

Students are now demanding a voice in determining what their education should include. In the old days, a student would simply drop out of school if he found that the narrowly prescribed, academically-oriented curriculum was not for him. Today, it is recognized that education is necessary for the economic competence needed to live a full life in this society. Young people, therefore, are following a different attack. If the curriculum does not speak to them, they don't drop out; they make demands for change. This is particularly true of young people of minority backgrounds who heretofore have simply let a stacked curriculum go unchallenged. They are serving notice that they will do so no longer.

When school opened in September 1968, student demonstrations forced the closing of three high schools in three different cities located near my own community of Berkeley. In each of these schools the Black Student Union presented demands for reform. The demands in these schools, and in others that were not closed, varied, but certain topics kept recurring. Central were the demands for curricular reform to include more black history and culture, for more black teachers and other certified staff members, and in general, for greater student influence on the life of the school. Each set of demands also contained other specifications that were mainly relevant to the local situation.

Across the Bay and down the peninsula from Berkeley, in a predominantly black high school in a black community set apart geographically by a freeway, the students went on strike demanding the resignation of the white principal and four or five white staff members. The principal was a liberal and strongly sympathized with the students' feelings. However, this was not a personal matter. It was instead a simple demand by black students that if they were to be isolated in a black school in a black community, then they at least wanted to have it run by a black principal. I empathized with the principal involved and recognized that although he had not created the circumstance, he was its victim. However, he was sufficiently objective to realize that this was not a personal attack, but a symbolic one, and he submitted his resignation, effective at the end of the year.

The impact of these racial demonstrations by the students in the surrounding area was not lost on the students of Berkeley.

Although Berkeley had stepped forward four years before with the desegregation of its junior high schools and had completed the process in 1968 by desegregating its elementary schools via two-way busing, Berkeley schools were not able to escape completely the tide of student militancy. Two or three weeks after school started, the Black Student Union of Berkeley High School held an unauthorized assembly and, after a series of meetings, developed a list of fourteen demands. I met with them, along with members of my staff and members of the Board of Education. A delegation of their leaders also appeared before the Board of Education in an open session to present their demands formally. Since the list of demands is fairly typical of the demands being made in most communities facing this challenge, I include the list here.

BLACK CURRICULUM

Preamble

The Black Student Union of Berkeley High School in order to promote pride in being Black, a knowledge of Black heritage and culture, to rid ourselves of the result of centuries of racial oppression in America, and to make the school curriculum relevant to the needs of Black people, do hereby make the following demands:

WE DEMAND   I.   A Black Curriculum Committee consisting of four Black students and three Black teachers.

WE DEMAND   II.   Student initiated courses. For every 30 students who sign an enrollment petition a course should be taught.

WE DEMAND   III. A Black Curriculum Coordinator responsible to the Black Curriculum Committee, who will also act as a personnel recruiter for Black teachers of Black courses.

WE DEMAND   IV.   The offering of the following courses as a part of the Black Curriculum.

A. Black American Literature and Poetry.

B. History of African Art, Literature, Culture, and Politics.

C. Black Journalism.

D. Black Socio-Economics.

E. Modern African Languages.
   1. Swahili
   2. Igbo

WE DEMAND   V.   The Black Curriculum Coordinator be given the authority to stock the school library with Black Literature as chosen by the Black students.

WE DEMAND   VI.   An in-service training program in Black American History and Culture for all teachers.

WE DEMAND   VII.   Five Black Counselors and we want them in two to four weeks.

WE DEMAND   VIII.   Two Black cooks and Soul food cooked three times a week in the school cafeteria.

WE DEMAND   IX.   African and Soul food must be included in the Food Classes.

WE DEMAND   X.   African dances must be included in the P.E. Curriculum.

WE DEMAND   XI.   The Tracking System of Berkeley High School must be eliminated.

WE DEMAND   XII.   All racists teachers and administrators be removed from our school.

WE DEMAND   XIII.   More Black teachers and administrators.

WE DEMAND   XIV.   Removal of law enforcement officers.

I will not go down the list point by point with an account of how we dealt with each demand. Suffice it to say we were able to implement many of them quickly. Many of the demands had already been put into operation or were already on the drawing board. Others had to be modified or postponed. However, the important thing was that we did establish quick contact with the students involved and demonstrated that we took their views seriously. In fact, I let it be known that some of these demands fell in the "why didn't I think of that myself?" category. An example is the offering of soul food as an optional item in the school cafeteria. We offer fish for Catholics on Friday. Why should we not make available to black students an item that is equally as important symbolically? The demand that racist teachers and administrators be removed from the school, however, was one which we had to temper considerably. Although we had taken a firm position that we would tolerate no discriminatory behavior on the part of any staff member, we did not want to become engaged in a witch-hunt regarding personal attitudes. We took the position that we would accept no list of names from groups of students. However, if an individual student felt he had been the victim of racist behavior, he or his parents could carry the matter to the principal and proceed through normal channels.

What was the upshot of all this? Of great importance is the fact that the demands were presented forthrightly. There was no student strike at Berkeley High School, and school continued to operate. I suspect that this was largely because in recent years Berkeley has been making giant strides both in ending racial isolation in the schools and in moving voluntarily to improve the curriculum. These steps have led to relatively good relations among races in this city. However, in spite of this good record, the Black Student Union demonstrated that we, too, were open to student militancy.

Although the examples of student militancy used here center largely around the racial issue, this phenomenon is by no means restricted to that subject. In the fall of 1968 the Student Action Movement, consisting primarily of Caucasian students, was formed and presented its own demands. Although this movement signified support of the Black Student Union, most of its demands centered around greater student involvement in the decision-making process. This type of movement will become increasingly common in the years ahead. No longer are students going to accept without question the irrelevancies that have been planned *for* them. Nor are they automatically going to defer to the authority figures the adult society has placed *over* them. This is a critical and questioning student generation. If something is wrong, it wants to know why, and why it cannot be corrected. In addition to this critical and questioning nature, however, I detect a strain of idealism and an unwillingness to go along with a hypocrisy simply because it is the line of least resistance. This is symbolized in many young people by a refusal to participate in the Pledge to the Flag on the grounds that the phrase "with liberty und justice for all" is simply not accurate.

Today's educator will have to accept the fact that students are insisting that they be more than just receptacles for a curriculum content that is planned *for* them. They are going to have a hand in the planning of their education—and in the shaping of society —whether we like it or not! True, this development has many pitfalls, but it is a desirable development (and one I like). It offers promise for the future and correction of inequities with which our generation has gone along for far too long. Student militancy is here and is going to increase. Our feelings about it are irrelevant. What we can do effectively to reach the students and work with them is the crucial question.

Teacher Militancy

Many of my observations concerning rising militancy in students can also be made about teachers. In fact, militancy among teachers has a somewhat earlier beginning than among students, but it has far from reached its peak. The day is long gone when the dedicated "school marm" would willingly devote countless extra hours to an underpaid job, and would not demean herself by haggling over money. Until recently, arbitrary administrators and school boards could bargain individually with each teacher—if, indeed, they bargained at all. It was more a case of the administrator simply informing the teacher sometime near the close of school whether or not he had a job for the next year. The teacher was supposed to accept this arrangement and to perform all the extra duties—teach oversize classes, chaperone extracurricular activities, and augment, from meager personal resources, shortages in the supplies needed for effective classroom work.

Teacher organization for purposes of effective bargaining is a post-World-War-II development. Early organization was difficult in this field, as in most others, because teachers who led this type of movement put their jobs on the line to do so. Those days, too, are rapidly disappearing. Now teacher organizations are an established part of the school scene, and most of the significant school districts have the machinery for some sort of collective negotiation, at least in the matter of salary and other teacher welfare concerns. However, teacher militancy goes considerably further. Teachers are now demanding a share in policy determination and in making decisions affecting the educational process. It is becoming an increasingly common occurrence at the opening of school to hear that districts in scattered parts of the country are not opening on schedule because of failure on the part of the teachers and boards of education to agree on conditions of employment.

In the fall of 1968, the largest school system in America was almost totally shut down by a strike affecting thousands of teachers and hundreds of thousands of students. In this instance, the typical items—salary, fringe benefits—were not even involved. The issue was the control of the school system. The union, despite its liberal position historically on such matters as integration and race relations, now found its own militancy severely challenged in defending certain of its members against the rising militancy of lay citizens in the community. The specific issue was whether or not the union can insist on its members retaining their assignments in the face of local community demands that they be transferred. Also at issue was the relative strength of the teaching staff and the lay members of the community in controlling the school and its curriculum. The results of this confrontation will doubtless influence similar situations as they develop in other cities.

Regardless of how the issues are joined or how settlements are reached in specific situations, one thing remains certain. The superintendent of today and tomorrow must accept rising teacher militancy as a fact of life. Teachers are not only going to be heard, they are going to be taken seriously. Their voice is going to be increasingly important in the determination of the policy and educational practices of a school district. Here again, although I may not like all the manifestation of this trend, I welcome the trend itself.

Community Militancy

If community militancy can be defined as pressure by lay citizens to affect the policies and practices of schools, it is not a new phenomenon. Middle- and upper-class citizens have been putting pressure, subtle and otherwise, on schools for years. It is no accident that, until the exposure of recent years, the better schools in town (those with better teachers, better and more plentiful equipment, and so forth) were generally those attended by students from influential families. Citizen pressure was more refined and couched in more polite, more genteel terms. However, the message came through. These middle- and upper-class citizens had the background to recognize good education and the verbal skill to articulate their desire for it for their children. If a given teacher failed to "reach" their children, the teacher and the school would hear about it.

In recent years such genteel pressure tactics have been matched by a rising tide of militancy on the part of individuals and groups who heretofore have not been taken seriously by the policy-making boards and professional establishments of typical school districts. This new wave of militancy, however, is not being expressed quite so politely. Direct action is the order of the day here, as with student militancy and teacher militancy. Parents are unhappy. Sit-ins and confrontations with staff members directly, in schools and before boards of education, occur more and more frequently. Demands are being made that schools correct defects and oversights in curricula, and that schools take seriously the obligation to educate *all* children. The new militants are determined that the society of the future will not be able to say about their children that the opportunities were there, but they lacked the education to take advantage of them. Basically, these militant community groups want "in" in areas which up to now have been closed to them.

Berkeley can serve as an example of community militancy, despite the fact that the militancy was largely in *support* of the school administration and the Board of Education as they proceeded with necessary educational and social change. This is in contrast to the pattern found in many other communities, where the militancy is directed against an establishment that is resisting change. Berkeley has had its share of delegations from the community coming before the Board of Education to recommend particular courses of action. These presentations have been more polite than in most communities, since this Board of Education for several years has been recognized by most Berkeleyans as one that is anxious to move forward. However, had this personal confidence in the good faith of the school board not existed, the community might have taken the same demanding militant stands as have other communities. Each of two citizens' committees that functioned in the late fifties and early sixties in the general area of race relations was preceded by presentations from civil rights groups requesting this type of study.

Similarly, in the spring of 1967, representatives of the black community, as well as white integrationists, joined the teacher organizations and pressed upon the school board the urgency of getting on with the task of elementary school integration. When the Berkeley Board of Education and school administration made a commitment to desegregate the schools and set a calendar for doing so, these militants were strong in their support and in their helpful advice during the development of the program to achieve the goal. Our Berkeley experience has demonstrated that community militancy need not be viewed as threatening, except by an administration and a board determined to maintain the status quo. I find it not only possible but highly desirable to work with militants in the community in developing a superior school system. This does not mean that every group or individual making a presentation before the board of education will achieve his total purpose. Many requests and demands will have to be postponed, altered, or even turned down. However, if the communication is present and if there is confidence in the good faith of a school administration and board, this type of militant, like the teachers and students I have discussed, can be allies in bringing about necessary and desirable change.

The educator must accept the fact that, whether he likes it or not, the community is going to be more militant in its demands than any in his experience to date. Militants from erstwhile disadvantaged groups are demanding their fair share in society. Schools are viewed as a tool in accomplishing this goal. Hence the attention is focused on schools. These militants are going to see that schools become part of the solution, rather than part of the problem. If this can be done politely, fine. However, our lay citizens have demonstrated by their presentations, their lists of demands, and their occasional resort to direct action, that they are to be taken seriously. If this cannot be accomplished politely, it will be done in other ways.

MILITANCY ANALYZED

I have discussed militancy here in the three categories: student, teacher, and community. These categories frequently can be conflicting. In New York in the fall of 1968 the militancy of the teachers and community militancy were in direct conflict over the share each was to have in the control of the schools. In other cases the demands of students conflict with what have been the prerogatives of teachers, or both students and teachers conflict with powerful factions of lay citizens. The educator will have to come to grips with each type of militancy and either reconcile or resolve differences as they arise. It is quite clear that militancy in all three groups is motivated by a desire for a greater piece of the action. Most of it is not directed primarily at a particular reform or a specific change, even though one of these appears to be the subject of a given confrontation. More basic is the desire of the students, teachers, and lay citizens to have a greater share in the decision-making power and in the process of policy determination.

All three categories of militants share the common attribute of being impatient of delay. They judge the merits of given situations, not by the progress that has been made, but by how far that progress still falls short of the ultimate goal. There is increasing reluctance to refer demands to committees for study. There is a greater insistence that legitimate goals be implemented immediately.

The militants of all three categories share general disillusion with the status quo and with the way "the establishment" has been running things. Tradition per se is becoming less and less acceptable as a reason for a given practice. When militants look around and see the inequities, they are sorely tempted to become cynical, not only about the status quo but also about those who have anything to do with it. Thus, the educator finds himself in danger of being distrusted simply because he is part of an establishment with which militants have become disillusioned.

What implications does militancy—by students, by teachers, and by members of the community—have for the educator? First, he must accept the reality of this militancy. It is here and will accelerate in intensity. It is both inevitable and legitimate in a free society. No educator who wants to remain relevant in the face of this militancy can be up tight about words such as *demands*. He must be sensitive to semantics and recognize that dealing with people who are not always polite does not necessarily represent capitulation. In fact, it is the only way that he can hope to make their contributions constructive.

Second, the educator must develop a greater sense of personal objectivity. This is difficult for anyone. No one likes to be barbed or personally insulted. However, the educator must recognize that the sometimes hostile attitude of militants is not to be taken personally.

Third, the educator must have the courage to say no when no is the correct answer. This takes courage and has risks, but when it is not even in the interest of the militants to give in to their demands, he must feel free to say so. The fact that it is sometimes necessary to say no makes it doubly important that he establish good working relations with militants and develop their confidence in his good faith.

Fourth and finally, the educator must be able to stimulate and direct militancy positively. He does not play one faction off against another. Rather, he attempts to stimulate and encourage each group to give positive support to education and work together for desired changes.

Today's militancy means that the educator must exercise greater leadership qualities than ever before. He can no longer speak from Olympus and expect to be followed unquestioningly. He must now take seriously the views of different segments of the school family and allow them a fair share in determining the direction education will take. No longer can he be a boss; he must be a leader.

14

The General Public

Reporting to the Stockholders

Today in America you have to sell your product if it is to be
supported by the general public. Using every medium of communication to get the facts to the public frequently and in an
attractive fashion is standard procedure for our friends in business and industry. Billions of dollars are spent in promoting new
products, and other billions in advertising old products. Industry
knows that you conduct aggressive selling campaigns or your
product is dead. Small and large industries alike invest from 5 to
15 percent of their income to sell and re-sell the product.

Education is America's biggest industry, something that must
be sold if we are to be sustained, and yet we allocate next to
nothing for reporting strengths and weaknesses to the stockhold-
ers. In many school districts the allocation *is* nothing—a big
zero. They not only ignore the item when they budget, but they
also ignore the entire selling process as far as personal effort is
concerned. My colleagues can list any number of reasons to
justify the existence of this situation.

We are so strapped for funds that every last dime must go to
activities that are mandated.

The Board of Education does not think it a proper use of local tax money.

No one in our county does it, and we don't want to be out of line.

Every last cent is earmarked for existing programs.

The local taxpayers' association would not approve.

We haven't the talent on our staff.

It is difficult, with existing monies, to just keep our heads above water.

If the people want to know what's going on in our schools, they can visit.

We would rather not tell them how bad things really are.

I say that it is time to change our course. We *must* get the word across to the local taxpayer that a greater dollar investment is necessary for education if we are going to survive. It *can* be done!

Let's focus on the district that will not—or cannot—allocate dollars for selling public education locally. It will be extremely difficult under these conditions, but you can still get the job done. Use every gimmick you have at your disposal: the school lunch menus (messages on the reverse side to mothers and dads); announcements at student activities; parent-teacher conferences; free guided tours for the taxpayers to see the physical condition of their schools (use the school buses for this, if necessary). Above all, get the parents to visit the schools. And when you get them there, go to work on them. Have carefully prepared reports, and give them the facts over and over and over again.

All those service clubs in town are always looking for a program; provide them with programs on a regular basis. Speak on the subject at the drop of a hat, and encourage other staff members to do the same (but make sure they have the facts). Ask the local teachers' association to kick in money to sponsor district-wide publications. The League of Women Voters and other civic organizations may have a printing press at their disposal; ask them to help.

Use the mass media. Radio and television are waiting for you to put them to work. Ask for editorials on behalf of the schools. Get on there yourself—and get the youngsters on. Call to the attention of the various stations the outstanding work being done by classroom teachers. (In Berkeley, I had my own so-called talk show. Actually, I did most of the listening. Citizens knew they could get my ear and chew me out, if they desired. But it was all free air time and I always found ways to get my message across.)

Don't neglect the newspapers. I am concerned about the poor image our schools have, but it is our fault, not the fault of the papers. They report what happens. Most of them will also report what we call to their attention. Prepare stories for them. Call them in to see all activities. Don't bury a story because it might make the school look bad; if you do, the reporters will never trust you again. Play it straight, and you can have a gold mine of free publicity.

Sure, it is hard work, but it is also fun. And more important, it works. I recall a situation in Maine in the mid-fifties resulting from Rudolph Fleschs's book, *Why Johnny Can't Read.* Everybody was up in arms because they had been told that their children could not read or spell. This was true throughout much of America, but it was not true in Sanford. I arranged programs all over town featuring children reading anything you gave them. And spelling was easy. I put the children on show again, and this time challenged the adults in the audience to join them. The children put the adults to shame! (We featured a little twelve-year-old girl, a sixth grader who had just won the state spelling championship.) The programs were a big hit; but, more important, word got around that Johnny could read and spell *if* he went to a public school in Sanford.

I also have been privileged to work with boards of education who supported the volunteer approach but also felt that this effort needed a little oomph, a touch of Madison Avenue; so they appropriated money to do those things that any successful company does. We hired layout people and artists and photographers and writers and put them on special projects. We had brochures, tabloids, and newsletters flowing almost weekly to either the total community or segments of the community. We had people writing material that could be enjoyed by college professors while others were writing for people who had grade school educations. We had newspapers geared to adult interests while others were written for young people. We had detailed reports beautifully illustrated on expensive paper while others went out carefully put together on cheap newsprint. But we communicated. At times we had direct mailings while at other times we had students hand deliver. *All* the people got the word, and got it often. (Was this the major reason why in twenty years my school districts never lost a tax election? In my opinion, yes!)

Communicating directly with the total public is mandatory, but our work requires much more than writing to them and talking to them. Involve them—that's the only way—and involve *all* of them. Go after the critics as well as those who support. Wilton needed a new school badly when I went there in 1948, and they had just been turned down by a close vote at a special town meeting. The school committee put their finger on the local butcher for the defeat. They were disturbed with Ralph. He opposed the school and he let every housewife hear why. I couldn't wait to involve old Ralph! I asked the school board to name a new building committee, and to put Ralph on the committee. He accepted and I went to work on Ralph. He got all the facts, not once, but over and over again. I encouraged him to come up with other answers or alternatives. He couldn't do it. Ralph became a supporter and we had our new school. (No, it doesn't always work out that way—but unless you involve them all, including the critics, you will never know.)

My main adversaries in Berkeley were the members of a Birch-oriented, far right group. We needed more money for our schools, and above all we needed community support. I encouraged the school board to name all sorts of ad hoc committees but always insisted that they include a cross section of the community (including this hard core opposition). Those who were asked to serve usually accepted with alacrity, did their homework, and every once in a while they supported a new program.

The key to the success of any committee can generally be traced to the chairman. Do not take a chance that the committee will pick the best qualified; instead, the board of education should hand pick this person in advance, making absolutely certain that the man can give this assignment the time it deserves. If he cannot, he is not the man.

Once the chairman has been selected and a committee has been formed that represents every last segment of the community, the ground rules must be established and spelled out in writing for the whole committee. Make certain that one thing is clear—the date they are expected to make their final report. Once the committee has been selected and the ground rules have been set, get out of the way; give them freedom to move in any direction they desire. And when the committee makes its report, do something about it, and do it immediately! Public involvement that does not end up with public action dooms citizens' participation and dooms public support of education at the same time. (If things are rotten in your city today, I'll bet you a buck that you have a dozen citizens' reports gathering dust in the board of education files. Want to bet?)

What about having outside consultants involved? I see a need, at times, for such special help. But when you spend taxpayers' money for such services, the people who put the money up have a right to know what the consultant said. Publish their recommendations. If they are critical, publish them! If they support your intuitive feelings, publish them! I strongly recommend making the public full time partners with the school administration and the board of education. Do not *occasionally* involve them —*always* involve them.

The schools belong to the people: young and old; those who support and those who attack; black and white; Protestant, Catholic, Jew, and agnostic. Respect them, consider them, love them, and involve them. Invite them all to participate as members of the team; establish priorities, goals, objectives, and ground rules; set the tone; establish the climate—and then turn them loose! A team of all the people is the most powerful and effective team of all.

15

The Superintendent and Politics

Participating in the Body Politic

The quality of the public schools at the local level is directly related to the amount of money made available for their support by those men and women who serve on local boards of education, city councils, and finance committees. At the state level quality is largely determined by those elected to the state legislature and by the governor of the state. The amount of federal money for the local schools is determined by the congressmen and senators we elect.

Almost without exception, each of these individuals must run for election. Collectively they spend millions of dollars on their campaigns. Individually a candidate spends amounts ranging from a few dollars to over a million. A successful campaign to win a board of education seat in Berkeley in the mid 1960s costs about $4,000 plus thousands of hours of time. The cost of winning a seat to Congress in the 7th Congressional District of California ranges from $13,465 to $25,588.

In 1966, Pat Brown, running for reelection as Governor, spent $2,154,822 in the primary and general elections, while his successful challenger reported expenditures of $3,498,026. Running for a second term for the California legislature in 1968 cost Democrat John J. Miller (former president of the Berkeley Board of

Education) an estimated $3,298. In 1964, Sherman Maisel (now a governor on the Federal Reserve Board) and Carol Sibley (long-time member of the Berkeley board) faced a tough recall election. Their supporters spent $12,000 to conduct a successful campaign, while the Parents' Association for Neighborhood Schools, conducting an unsuccessful campaign, also spent a sizable figure.

Winning any election today takes a spirited, dedicated, and well-financed organization. In the course of the campaign the candidate makes promises and pledges (some of which he will probably keep) and he comes in contact with thousands of people. Some of these people he meets briefly to say hello and to ask for their support. From others he seeks advice. He would like the open support of everybody, but he knows that this is impossible.

During this period when the candidate is open to public scrutiny, he may be forced to take positions on current issues. What do schoolmen do about this situation? Do they ask these candidates to take positions on such questions as decentralization, integration, and dollar support? Do they ask to meet the candidate privately to let him know what the needs and challenges are? Do they ask the candidate what he will do about the problems, once elected?

Some school administrators do all of these things, and more. But most of them run and hide until the election is over; then they come out of hiding and make whatever adjustments are required of them by the winner. Could this be one of the reasons that elected officials refuse to turn to schoolmen for advice on school questions after their election? Of course! Could this be one of the reasons that the downtown merchants and the local teamsters, both groups involved in the election, have a greater pull on the winner as decisions are made? Of course! Could this be one of the reasons that elected officials sometimes totally ignore educational problems? Of course! Could this be why education often comes last when the funds are divided? You bet!

I am not suggesting that every administrator become personally involved or go out on a limb to support publicly his candidate in every election. I am saying that schoolmen should reach
every candidate before the election to let him know what the
schools need and to ask him what he intends to do about these
problems if elected.

There was no question in my mind about the importance for
public education of the 1966 gubernatorial election in the Golden
State. Ronald Reagan had made it clear from the very beginning:
"The state's responsibility for education should not extend below grade one." He promised to cut taxes, local and state, and
this meant one thing: reduced services and less education for all
California children. On the other hand, Pat Brown had promised
to extend the privileges of a public education to all children four
years of age and over, and had indicated that more state aid was
essential for public schools.

What does a schoolman do in an election like this, when he
knows that education for all children at the age of four is mandatory if equal educational opportunities are to be a reality? What
does he do when he also knows that local dollars have dried up,
that teachers are underpaid, that classes are too large, and that
schools are badly in need of repair? My colleagues in California
—most of them, not all of them—clammed up! They reacted as
they had traditionally over the years. They abstained! They hid!
They refused to become involved in politics!

I was asked to join the Brown team as an educational advisor
and I jumped at the opportunity. I worked after hours, in the
evenings, on weekends, and grew to admire Pat Brown. On
election night, when the votes clearly indicated Mr. Reagan was
the winner, I was a disappointed man. But at least I had tried—
I had participated—I had worked. There was satisfaction in
knowing that I had made every effort to support Pat Brown's
stand on school needs.

In the race for the presidency in 1968, I worked openly for the late Senator Robert F. Kennedy from the moment he announced his candidacy. I had been privileged to know Senator Kennedy intimately and was fully cognizant of his total commitment to excellence in our schools. When I received a call from Senator Kennedy's close confidant (and my old friend from Prince Edward days) William vanden Heuvel, asking, "In your position as Berkeley's school superintendent would you take an active part in the California campaign?" my answer was a quick, resounding, "Just give me the opportunity!"

That's all it took. Thomas Braden, president of the State Board of Education and foe of Max Rafferty, took over the RFK campaign in California and called me immediately. My involvement consisted of making public appearances in support of Senator Kennedy, having parties in my home, and acting as Alameda County fund raising chairman for the campaign. The response of the Berkeley *Gazette* was a roaring editorial attacking me for being involved in a political campaign.

Editorial

Questionable Actions of Superintendent Sullivan

If we did not know better, we would think Berkeley Superintendent of Schools Neil V. Sullivan is taking his cues from State Superintendent of Public Instruction Max Rafferty.

Dr. Sullivan has, on numerous occasions, taken public pot shots at Rafferty for debasing his high trust of state-wide public education by playing politics.

We were, therefore, quite shocked last week to learn Dr. Sullivan has endorsed Sen. Robert F. Kennedy's bid for the presidency and is actively supporting the senator, even to the point of soliciting funds. Sullivan also endorsed one of the candidates for Alameda County Supervisor.

Aside from many minor objections which could be raised to Sullivan's actions, the Gazette has two major criticisms:
—Neil V. Sullivan—the man—cannot be disassociated from Neil V. Sullivan—the appointed public official.

—It is highly unethical for any appointed public official to enter the political arena.

Dr. Sullivan is one of the best known public educators in the nation and certainly the best known in northern California. The very fact he made an endorsement, made it news, and therefore, negates Sullivan's contention he is acting as a private citizen.

When one becomes well known because of dramatic innovations in his work, then, at the public level, the man and his work are synonymous.

For Dr. Sullivan to run up the banner of the rights of the individual citizen is a facade which is fanciful, if not farcical.

It is a long established and well grounded unwritten law, that public officials, appointed by elected officials remain silent on partisan politics—particularly on candidates for election.

By observing this practice appointed officials avoid entering the gray area of confusing the public good with personal gain.

If one doubts the propriety of this long established rule of thumb, one should contemplate the sticky aftermath which would follow other appointed officials endorsing candidates.

What would the public think and how would it react if Police Chief William P. Beal or City Manager William Hanley endorsed political candidates?

Berkeley *Daily Gazette,* June 3, 1968

I was not surprised by the *Gazette* attack nor was I deterred in my efforts. Being criticized by the *Gazette* was nothing new to me nor was it particularly disturbing. The day the editorial appeared, I received a call from one of northern California's brightest young lawyers, congratulating me for my willingness to support Senator Kennedy, assuring me that my political activities were perfectly legitimate, and indicating that he had put a generous campaign contribution in the mail for Senator Kennedy. He also stated that he had written a letter to the editor of the *Gazette,* in which he cited the legal grounds for my participation in a political campaign. (It is interesting to note that this letter was received in the Berkeley *Gazette* office on June 6, 1968.

Weeks passed before it was printed; the lawyer was told the original letter was lost. He sent another copy to the editor.)

> Mike Culbert's Monday editorial comment regarding Sullivan the man and Sullivan the superintendent compels me to congratulate you upon taking a public position in support of Senator Robert Kennedy. The safe and easy course for any appointed public official is to avoid partisan comment and commitment. Perhaps that is the basic weakness in our system of administration of public affairs.
>
> The law of California expressly permits school district employees to engage in political activity, subject to certain appropriate restrictions, and thereby encourages them to fulfill their role as citizens in a participatory democracy. For public employees to speak out on vital issues and in support of candidates for elective office requires far more courage than is required for them to remain silent. Your bold, courageous action will assist immeasurably in bringing to the attention of the community the views and opinions of our highly-trained and knowledgeable public servants concerning the really vital issues of this frightening and challenging age in which we live.

I would like to take you back for a look at another election. When I was in my first superintendency in the Jay-Wilton area of Northwest Maine (in the beautiful Rangely lakes area), the Republicans had controlled the State House for eighty-three years. Only one Democrat had been elected governor of Maine since the Civil War. Public education was a poor stepchild in the state's family. A young Watersill attorney, a Democrat who had been elected to the state legislature in 1947, announced his candidacy for governor. He had fought for greater state aid and had suggested a complete reorganization of the State Board of Education and State Department of Education. His name was Edmund Muskie. Ed Muskie was elected and the children of Maine had a friend in the State House. This sensitive, creative young leader was to move education ahead in Maine by leaps and bounds.

Did my support of Robert F. Kennedy in the California primary of 1968 and Edmund S. Muskie for Governor of Maine in 1955 have a direct effect on their election? I doubt it very much. They were outstanding individuals and would have won anyway. Supporting candidates means, however, that I can call to their attention programs that I feel are important to education. Does this mean that all my programs will be supported? Certainly not! All it means is that my suggestions will be given a fair hearing—the same fair hearing such men would give any suggestion. *But*, being known by an office holder does help to expedite the suggestions reaching his desk.

Enough about major state and national elections. Let's look at local elections. School administrations go through at least one election annually. I seem to be saying hello and goodbye to school board members continually. Generally, I have been able to remain neutral as the city voted on the question of who would serve as their representative on the local board, because I have served in communities where highly qualified candidates sought office on a non-political basis. I also have been privileged to have active chapters of the League of Women Voters on the scene. Their exhaustive efforts have given all candidates equal exposure, and I have been confident of the results. (I also learned early as a school superintendent that a candidate critical of the operation of the public schools could become a positive force as a new board member.)

I mentioned earlier the recall election in Berkeley in 1964. That election was something very special. Two of the original incumbents who had brought me to Berkeley were being challenged by two candidates sponsored by the Parents' Association for Neighborhood Schools. An incumbent victory meant that I would continue to have a pro-integration school board, a board committed to a search for excellence in public education. A victory for the Parents' Association for Neighborhood Schools meant an end to any move toward integration.

What does the local superintendent do in a situation like this? I campaigned for the incumbents and I made my position clear. A victory for the challengers meant that I would pack the next day and leave; the superintendency could then be turned over to someone who could live under a different philosophical climate. An incumbent victory meant that I would stay in Berkeley and redouble my efforts for school integration. The people of Berkeley settled the question by decidedly reelecting the incumbents. (See Neil V. Sullivan, *Now Is the Time*, Bloomington: Indiana University Press, 1970.)

I grow tired of hearing some of my colleagues criticize the actions of elected groups. Why should they criticize? They sat on the sidelines during the elections! They deserve what happens when they are careful not to commit themselves in any way on any issues.

I flare up when people tell me that I should not lower myself by becoming involved in politics. Lower myself? Hardly! I react strongly when I am told that politics is a dirty game. This unfortunate image has been created by *some* politicians who are indeed dirty people and who use tactics that are unacceptable in any cause. It is true, unfortunately, that there have been times and places in our history when corrupt administrators defiled our whole society. But these have been exceptions rather than the rule. Involvement in politics does not necessitate the use of questionable techniques. Politics are rough, tough, and trying, but not necessarily dirty. I have never felt cleaner in my life than after my visits with Senator Edward Kennedy or Senator Robert Kennedy, or when George Willard or Carol Sibley or Alberta Saletan (school board presidents) visited me.

I also do not accept the theory that a candidate becomes indebted to this person or that person involved in an election. This has not been my experience at all. On several occasions the candidate I supported was defeated. The winner did not freeze me out or turn down my district merely because I supported his opponent. Berkeley received hundreds of thousands of dollars in special aid annually from Sacramento following Pat Brown's defeat, despite my open opposition to the Reagan-Rafferty administration. I did and do differ with them politically and philosophically, but these men have been honest in their handling of requests from the various cities and towns in California. I never worried that Berkeley students and teachers would suffer the loss of state or federal funds because of my political activities. I was confident that my staff was the most creative in California and our projects the most imaginative. I was certain that no matter who was in Sacramento, Berkeley would do all right on special projects, as well as on general aid, for which funds are carefully allocated on the basis of a state formula. I had the same confidence in the ability of my staffs in New York and Maine. (In Virginia I dealt with the Foundations.)

My rationale for participating in politics, therefore, is not simply to influence our political leaders to make more funds available for the city or town where *I serve* as superintendent. It is far deeper than that!

First, I see no reason for abstaining merely because I am a school man. Rather, I feel that *because* I am a school man I am better qualified than many other Americans to judge critical questions facing America. My undergraduate and graduate days were spent studying social and educational issues. My experiences since leaving the university campus have exposed me daily to the critical issues of society and the problems of cities, towns, and suburbs. Why not use this education and experience to help influence others to elect the best qualified individuals?

Second, I am constantly telling young people to become involved, to stand up on issues, to be heard. How could they believe me if I did not demonstrate, by my own actions, that I mean what I say? If it is true that the youth of 1970 have lost respect for people of my generation—and it is obvious that many have—then let us examine and re-examine those of our practices that caused this breach between the generations. Can our youth look at the people who administer their schools and say, "He is a person I can admire. He speaks out on controversial issues. I don't always agree with him, but I know where he stands"—or do they look at us and shake their heads, bewildered by our vacillation and procrastination?

Third, while my involvement may not necessarily mean extra money for our local schools, it may mean better education for all children, and that is my objective—better conditions in Watts (Los Angeles), Hunters Point (San Francisco), Harlem (New York City), and the many other places where vast improvement is so desperately needed.

I urge school men to become active participants in the political arena. Only when they do, will educators' voices be heard in the legislative halls of the state capitol and in Congress. Only if we immerse ourselves in the critical issues of our time will our work be recognized as dignified and significant by the law-makers. Let us stop dodging issues, and face them! Let's stop chickening out on our responsibilities, and share with other aggressive and responsible groups in the choice of our political leaders.

16

Support for Education

Obtaining the Wherewithal

It was 1952 and I was in Cleveland, Ohio, attending a regional meeting of the American Association of School Administrators. The speaker that evening was the young senator from California, Richard Nixon, the Republican candidate for the Vice-Presidency of the United States. I had listened to him give the "broad brush" treatment to a variety of subjects. He carefully avoided specifics on his position on federal aid to education. The audience had a chance to ask the candidate a few questions, and I candidly asked, "Where is the money going to come from to improve conditions in our local schools?"

Mr. Nixon: "Public education is a local responsibility and the money for its support must be raised by your local school board." That November Mr. Nixon was elected Vice-President and Dwight Eisenhower was our new President. The new Vice-President kept his promise and for the next eight years school superintendents fought valiantly to find the money on the home front.

A small breakthrough occurred, however, in October 1957, when Russia launched Sputnik I. Suddenly America was up tight over the situation, realizing that we were not number one in the race for the control of outer space. It looked at that time as though we were a poor second and our national leaders had to find an immediate scapegoat. The finger was placed on public education and the nation was told that our public schools had failed to provide our students with proper skills in math and science. At about the same time, a best-selling book, *The Ugly American*, written by William J. Lederer and Eugene Burdick, a University of California professor, described the typical American living outside our shores, revealing his inadequate educational background, particularly in handling a second language.

As usual, Congress reacted in panic and quickly enacted the National Defense Education Act providing $30 million the first year (and now providing about $200 million annually) for improvement of programs in mathematics, in science, and in foreign languages, and, in addition, offering some assistance for counseling services. But in order to receive a grant from Washington, a local school district had to put up a matching amount of money.

That year I was serving as school superintendent on the north shore of Long Island—the gold coast—and had in my districts parts of such communities as Old Westbury (home of the Vanderbilts), East Williston, Roslyn Heights, and Mineola. The district was a tremendously wealthy one and the school budget was generally approved, without debate, by landslide majorities. Finding local dollars to match federal dollars posed no particular problem in such a district. Actually, the district had done an outstanding job in developing innovative programs in science and math, had a very low pupil-counselor ratio, had introduced foreign languages in the elementary schools, had purchased the latest electronic equipment, and, in general, had no monetary problems. But the new money was there, and we went after it with real gusto. I can recall seeing huge new television sets in every classroom—very nice—but educational TV was still years away, so the sets were rarely used. (A few citizens complained when their children came home and reported that they had watched the World Series in school that day.) As a result of the new federal money, the rich district I was supervising became richer and the poor districts became poorer. Tragically, most of the nation's children attend school in our large cities where extra dollars to match new federal money simply do not exist.

Let's be very specific. The student-counselor ratio in my district was 200 to 1. It was 2,000 to 1 in some other areas, and in some school systems there was no counseling service at all. Let's take foreign languages. We were offering French, Latin, Spanish, German, and had just introduced Russian, while a neighboring poor district was struggling to offer French and Spanish.

I was critical of the National Defense Education Act for more than one reason. The nation had quickly evaluated our science program and Congress had reacted. But there was no evaluation of our program in the arts and the humanities; the sad condition of these programs in most public school systems went unnoticed and was ignored by our federal government. The Act did nothing to equalize educational opportunities. It told Americans that to the federal government the important part of our education was in the area of science. "Face saving" in science appeared more important than developing students who were well rounded, achieving human beings, doing their thing in a manner they understood and accepted, and above all, participating in the planning of events reflecting their interests. This suggested to me that our schools and our students were being used as pawns in the cold war.

The history of federal support is closely tied to programs that tend to buttress our ability to make war. The Smith-Hughes Act of 1917 was aimed at developing and speeding up vocational training courses during World War I. Once initiated, federal funds continued to support a very worthwhile program—but I raise the question again: what about the arts and the humanities?

During the exciting years of the Kennedy administration, the young President provided spirited leadership for cross-section support of all educational programs. He was particularly sensitive to the need to correct conditions in our inner-city schools, to retrain the displaced and the unemployed, to feed the poor, to provide needed health services in our schools, and to provide monies for improved teaching of the arts and the humanities. His efforts for two and one-half years met with hairline defeats in Congress. He did, however, see a major educational bill of his pass. (Ironically, it was signed by the young President just a short time before his assassination.) What area had Congress again reacted to? You guessed it—vocational education. I feel strongly that the primary motivating influence on Congress at that time had been the Cuban missile crisis.

Following the death of John Fitzgerald Kennedy, the Johnson administration succeeded in passing the first general aid to education bill—the Elementary-Secondary Education Act of 1964— a truly admirable piece of legislation that pumped one billion dollars a year into our public schools and libraries for regional planning, for research, and for innovation at all levels, with additional support for state departments of education. President Johnson had fulfilled his pledge to the nation. When he succeeded Mr. Kennedy he promised to push through Congress those programs the young President had fought so hard to implement.

Looking at the Elementary-Secondary Education Act, one had to admit that Congress finally passed a bill that attempted to provide a minimum of equality in our nation's schools. Most of the money is found in Title I, which provides financial support for school children whose parents fall within the poverty range.

The amount of money appropriated by Congress is extremely beneficial; instead of receiving 2 or 3 percent federal support, a poor district might receive as much as 7 or 8 percent—but this is still only a drop in the bucket. The local district must now find that other 92 to 95 percent. Does the Elementary-Secondary

Education Act bring poor schools up to any sort of minimum? Certainly not! So the story remains basically the same: turn to the state and to local government.

Turning to the state has become almost as frustrating as turning to the federal government, with a few notable exceptions. I single out in this exemplary category the state of New York. Here is a state that has a remarkable history, starting with the administration of Alfred E. Smith in 1918. That able governor was responsive to the needs of local government and introduced the "partnership principle" in state-community relationships. A minimum program was spelled out and the state agreed to underwrite 50 percent of the cost, with additional equalization help to the poorer districts. As a result of that historic agreement, New York's public schools soared far above those in other states. Strong state support was coupled with a remarkably responsive state board of education and with strong state superintendents of schools appointed by the state board.

The beautiful marriage between state and local government continued under Franklin D. Roosevelt, Herbert H. Lehmen, Averell Harriman, and on into the Nelson A. Rockefeller administration starting in 1963. However, Mr. Rockefeller, in his first two years as governor, refused to push for the higher taxes that were needed to maintain the partnership principle. As a result, local districts were forced either to increase their effort to maintain programs or to hold the tax line, cut back in services, and hold the line on teacher salaries.

A wild roar went up in the Empire State. Mr. Rockefeller had decided, in the meantime, to be a candidate for the Presidency in 1964. His campaign took him from state to state, and following him everywhere he went, like Mary's little lamb, were militant groups of New York educators carrying placards reminding him that he had reneged on the partnership principle and condemning him for his action. Mr. Rockefeller got the message. He changed his position, and in 1965 state taxes were raised and the state share of public support was increased. I was in New York during that time.

I was in California in 1966 during the race for the governorship of that state. The record will show that under Pat Brown the state maintained its so-so effort to support public education. This so-so effort should not be scoffed at, however. We must keep in mind the burgeoning school population in California; just staying even in public education was taking annual increases of millions of dollars. But Governor Brown tried. New money was found for programs to care for the mentally and physically handicapped, for the slow and retarded learner, and for the high-potential child. Governor Brown succeeded in raising taxes for improved public schools, but despite these Herculean efforts, the overall percentage of support from the state slipped drastically.

I shouted; I protested; I wrote articles; I talked on the radio; I appeared before citizens' committees urging California to move toward the partnership program. Who heard me? Governor Brown not only heard me, but he also asked me to join his team. (I think you should know that I was not a Brown fan when I went to California. I had been disturbed in 1960 when Mr. Brown was reluctant to support Mr. Kennedy in that campaign. How do I explain the change in my attitude? Simple: Pat Brown was more concerned about people and about consistency and honesty than he was about being elected a third time as California's governor. Certainly, he wanted a third term, but he knew that with a continually expanding population he would be a bold-faced liar to suggest that taxes could be reduced without also curtailing services.)

Governor Brown asked me about equalizing educational opportunities (one of his goals), and I reported that such conditions would never exist until all children were given the same educational opportunities *before* the age of six. Yes, this meant public kindergartens at five and nursery schools at four and preferably at three.

The battle lines were never clearer than in the 1966 race for the governorship of California. Mr. Brown made it clear that he would work for increased state aid for public schools and came out in support of free public education beginning at age four. The hero of the class B movies, Ronald Reagan, promised the 20 million Californians that he would reduce taxes. How did the California election of 1966 come out? My candidate was not even close. The people elected the Hollywood star as their new leader.

Today in America, school superintendents find it increasingly difficult to get *new* money from the state capitals. Generally speaking, the money we have received has been based on formulas developed a decade ago, with small new incentive grants covering special programs during their first two or three years of operation. The state further complicates things for local administrators when the aid program is based on the previous year's expenditures and enrollment.

The real hangup comes when state legislative bodies decide to mandate new programs. I recognize the right of the state to do this, but I vehemently protest its giving the mandate to the local districts unaccompanied by the financial support needed to carry out that mandate. I could cite innumerable examples of this irresponsible behavior but one should suffice.

In 1961 the California legislature mandated that foreign language was required for all students in grades seven and eight, but did not provide any *new* money to local school districts for the required courses. School districts with restricted incomes were forced to water down or completely eliminate other courses in order to provide monies for foreign languages. Unfortunately, the electives were hardest hit, particularly the fine arts program. In addition, class size had to be increased in major subject matter fields, resulting in a further cheapening of an already meager program. Here again, the rich districts were able to make the adjustment, while the average and poor districts did more belt tightening.

One other negative aspect of a mandate program should be pointed out. Where would local school superintendents find the thousands of new teachers required to teach the new courses? The rich districts spent thousands of dollars recruiting in other parts of the country, while the average and poor districts juggled credentials of available staff and assigned poorly prepared staff members to the new teaching assignments.

Seven years later the state reversed itself and freed local districts almost completely from state requirements governing subject matter to be taught, length of periods, and course offerings during a week, month, or semester.

The typical school superintendent has little or no effect upon decisions made in the United States Congress, and this holds true also at the state level. However, a dynamic state commissioner of education, with the help of various educational groups, including the local superintendents, can exert a powerful influence on the state legislature and the governor. This is done very successfully in New York, where all interested groups work together. Parent-teacher associations, the New York State Teachers' Association, university professors, and New York school boards meet regularly to determine priorities and then to address the legislature as one solid, powerful, united front.

New York's practice is not followed in many states, unfortunately, and education runs a poor second or third when the money is being allocated in the state capitol. Why is this so? The major reason is that few states can boast of a truly strong state department of education, with a top notch state superintendent of schools. It is important to point out that part of the success of the state of New York is due to the fact that politics plays no part in the selection of the members of the state board of education, and that this highly ethical board then appoints the state commissioner of education. In California, you find that the state board of education is appointed by the governor, and depending on who that governor is, the appointments can be entirely political. Mr. Reagan in his selection, for example, leaned strongly toward conservative Republicans, while Mr. Brown selected individuals who were, by and large, Democrats and liberals.

The real problem in California comes, however, when the people, at a popular election every four years, select the state superintendent. As a result, the position becomes a political one, not an educational one. A campaign is conducted; the candidate who can attract the largest financial support, making it possible for him to use radio and TV, purchase newspaper space, control billboards, hire a large staff to handle promotion, and have an airplane at his disposal to move quickly from one end of the state to the other, is going to win. Max Rafferty, winner in 1966, had no difficulty with his budget. Right wingers saw to it that he had whatever money was needed to win. Because of this, Mr. Rafferty had only token opposition from men who were not known, and never became known, outside of their local districts. The race for the superintendency in 1966 in California was no race at all.

So we look to the nation's capital for help and it comes spasmodically, unevenly, and for limited programs only. We turn to the states and find a "hold the line" attitude prevalent. We check income carefully, and, depending entirely upon the state we are in, we will be fortunate indeed if we can secure 40 percent of our funding from the state and federal governments. This means that we must find 60 percent or more at the local level.

Before we zero in on the local tax dollar, we make every effort to involve private foundations in our problems. We go the route —Rockefeller Foundation, Ford Foundation, Rosenberg Foundation, Kellogg Foundation, Carnegie Foundation—and plead our case. Competition for available dollars is keen and we must be very skillful in presenting our case, and have a particularly innovative and creative project or we are doomed to failure.

SUPPORT FOR EDUCATION 161

When I left Berkeley in 1969, we were operating innumerable programs financed by the foundations. We not only had large grants from the Carnegie, Rockefeller, and Ford Foundations, but we also had equally important help from the B'nai B'rith Anti-Defamation League Fund for Action on Continuing Education (known as FACE). Berkeley had won national acclaim for its innovative programs, and I used whatever influence I had to encourage the foundations to turn it on for Berkeley—and turn it on they did. In addition to the private foundation route, we approached other state and federal agencies. An example would be the United States Civil Rights Office. We felt our efforts in school integration merited financial support from them. We said so; we worked on it; our efforts were rewarded handsomely. We successfully brought in millions of dollars for new Berkeley programs and other millions to buttress on-going programs.

But there is a catch to this sort of help: it is terminal. A day of reckoning for the local district comes when the funding expires, and expire it will—maybe in a year, possibly two, rarely beyond three. Then the district must decide whether or not the program should be continued. Pressure groups go to work and wheels turn. Generally the new program wins support, but something must be trimmed because now local dollars must be allocated.

Local dollars—that is where the bite comes. School superintendents are finding that getting more money from the local property tax borders on the impossible. To put it succinctly, we went to the cupboard and the cupboard was bare. Why? Because the burgeoning costs of running a school district simply cannot be supported by a system that depends on increasing the local property tax. You can only stretch elastic so far and you can only push property taxes so far; both have a breaking point. That breaking point has been reached with the home owners. They cannot afford a greater tax increase on their homes and, fortunately for them and unfortunately for school superintendents and the children in the schools, the taxpayer in most situations has the last word. That last word comes at tax election time when local citizens decide whether or not they will vote in favor of more money for the operation of the public schools.

A few years ago—in the middle sixties—I was offered a lucrative contract by the Detroit Board of Education and turned it down. Why? I had been deeply impressed by the caliber of person I found on the Detroit Board of Education. I wanted to go to one of our very largest cities and work on the educational problems confronting its schools, *but* I knew that in order to be successful, I would need minimal financial support at the city level. The crucial question was whether or not the Detroit voter would provide me with that support. The answer was given to me by the voters at the same time that I was offered a contract. The people of Detroit had been asked to increase the tax rate so that additional monies would be provided for the public schools, and on the same day, to approve a bond issue for the establishment of a free junior college system. The voters went to the polls knowing that the teachers were threatening to strike if their salary demands were not met. The voters were also fully aware that Northern High School, a predominantly black school, was closed by a student strike. If they had done their homework, they would have learned that teachers were not only unhappy about their salary levels, but equally unhappy about such vital things in their schools as large pupil-teacher ratios, inadequate supplies and lack of instructional equipment, dilapidated school plants, and little attention to broad summer school programs and programs to meet the needs of the educationally handicapped children.

The scene was set. Political leaders, including Mayor Jerome Cavanagh, and black and white leaders were solidly behind the board's request for additional monies. They voted in large numbers in Detroit on that election day, and on the question of whether or not they would increase their property tax to provide additional monies for support of their public schools, they voted overwhelmingly in opposition to the increase. The Detroit incident was repeated in city after city and today it is unusual to see a school tax election pass.

In 1968 the situation in most California cities was acute. Major cities like Los Angeles and Oakland had a dismal record and they dared not go back to the local people to ask for more money. They had tried several times and their efforts had ended in defeat. Now they turned, with support from California's other major cities, to the state. There was a bill before the legislature that would provide immediate help to the state's largest cities. A meeting was arranged with the governor. The dimension of the problem and the seriousness of the situation were carefully spelled out. The governor's attention was called to the problems of the inner-city schools, the physical condition of the school facilities, the overcrowded buildings and classrooms, the underpaid staff.

Governor Reagan listened respectfully, then made his recommendation and stated his position. He would not support the bill calling for new monies, but he was reported to have suggested: "Direct the teachers to come back to the school on weekends, and yes, after school, and go to work correcting the condition. Give them paint brushes, saws, have them provide the labor and correct the situation." Unfortunately, our governor failed to tell us where we were to find the paint and who would donate the lumber.

Detroit exploded in the summer of 1967 and disturbances occurred in every major city in our country. Governor George Romney and Detroit's mayor, Jerome Cavanagh, appeared on national TV and stated "We did everything we could. We can't understand how this happened." Yes, Governor, you and Mayor Cavanagh may have done everything possible, but the facts of the matter are that the system is structured for the strangulation of our public schools unless drastic changes are made in how they are financed.

The money cannot be found, in the typical community, from the local property tax. The money can be found in most states if legislatures have the courage to enact a taxing program that equitably shares the responsibility with the people, business, and industry; however, I am not optimistic about state politicians demonstrating the leadership required for a state to assume the necessary responsibility for adequate tax support of public education.

So we turn to Washington. I see here an answer to our tax dilemma and, at the same time, the possibility of providing equal educational opportunities in all of the fifty states. The broad taxing power of our federal government can be used to turn up the necessary dollars. In addition, those political leaders who make the decisions are far enough away from home so that they can make their decisions without being threatened by defeat at the next election.

I strongly recommend that we continue to use the local property tax as one source of funds for public education. Why? Because people will remain closer to their schools if they can see how a portion of their local tax dollar is tied directly to the quality of their public schools.

I feel the same way about state support. Public education is a state responsibility; therefore, the state should be a full partner in the support of public education—not contributing picayune support, but putting up 50 percent of the cost.

In the end, however, the federal government must help provide the balance. Why is balance necessary? Simply because some communities and some states have tremendous potential to support a quality program while a neighboring city or state has no such ability and, as a result, provides second-rate educational services for its children.

In 1968, New York was spending $200 more per pupil than its sister state of California. Let's project this to a twenty-room elementary school and see what this means. First, a typical classroom of thirty-five students and one teacher: thirty-five times $200 results in $7,000 more for one classroom and teacher in New York than in California. In a twenty-room school, the amount would be $140,000 more. The school principal in New York has many desirable options open to him: smaller classes, special teachers, more supplies, better equipment, higher salaries. All of this means improved staff and student morale and a better teaching-learning climate.

Now let us look at two cities in the Bay Area of Northern California. The cost per pupil in Berkeley is $1,089, while in Oakland it is $800 (projected figures for 1969). Berkeley's additional money provides a rich high-potential program, compensatory education, teacher aides, smaller classes, a rich elective program, buses for school integration, an extensive program for the educationally handicapped, remedial programs, enrichment programs, and, in general, a quality integrated program. Are you surprised when I tell you that one of Berkeley's major problems was limiting enrollment in the city schools to children of parents who legally resided in Berkeley? You shouldn't be! If you lived in Oakland, you would have known how impossible the conditions were in your schools. You would also have known that the educational grass just one block away was vibrant and green. You might have been so frustrated that you would be tempted to break the law by falsely registering your child in the neighboring school district. Many people did just that!

This imbalance has continued: a rich district and a neighboring poor district; a rich state and a neighboring poor state (and most states are far poorer than California)—all in the business of educating children; one properly financed, another immersed in problems because of inadequate funding. The well financed district should be expected to turn out successful, achieving students, who probably will end up being successful adults. The district with restricted funds will probably turn out thousands of under-achievers, who have been given a one-way ticket to failure and second-class citizenship in our competitive society.

A country dedicated to freedom and equality for all of our children cannot permit the circumstances that result in inequality to continue.

17

Los Angeles Courthouse

A Career Cross-examined

CRAWFORD v. BOARD OF EDUCATION

It had been a long, trying two days in the Los Angeles County Courthouse. I had been on the stand for ten demanding hours. What was I doing there? This case interested me, and the attorney for the American Civil Liberties Union felt my testimony would be valuable. The defendant in this case was the Los Angeles Board of Education, trying desperately, but skillfully, to head off a court decision that would result in the integration of the public schools. I was satisfied that my testimony would help convince the presiding superior court judge, Alfred Gitelson, that the Los Angeles Board of Education had indeed injured tens of thousands of children by permitting de facto segregation to exist in that city of millions.

I was satisfied that I had the opportunity to tell it like it was. I was tired of hearing my fellow superintendents procrastinate and vacillate on this vital subject of school integration. I was disturbed by conditions as they exist in our urban communities. I was tired of waiting patiently for action to be taken voluntarily by Northern cities to integrate the schools, and disturbed because of the lack of action by boards of education. I had observed the patient minorities wait for fourteen long years to see tangible results from *Brown* v. *Board of Education,* the 1954 Supreme Court decision on de jure segregation. I was disturbed because virtually nothing had occurred in Los Angeles that would reflect compliance with the law, and there was increasing evidence that the "establishment" had no intention of implementing the law. Because of the lack of action, explosions were occurring in our public institutions, from Roxbury, Massachusetts, to the campus of San Francisco State College.

The Kerner-Lindsay Committee, asked by President Johnson to report on the causes of the riots in our cities, had reported clearly and succinctly that the cause of the tensions in our society and of the violence on city streets, in our schools, and on our campuses could be traced to the racist tendencies and characteristics of white America. The report was definite and specific, and the recommendations were as clear as the air on a newborn day in the High Sierras. But the President of the United States remained unbelievably silent—perhaps because he was a "lame duck President," and his support could only have ignited the tinderbox conditions existing in city after city, from Boston to Seattle.

I was also disturbed because the Democratic candidate for the presidency had refused to take on Mayor Daley and his Chicago police force for their sadistic attack on the young and misguided militant students during the Democratic convention. I was equally disturbed with the incoming President, Richard Nixon, for his refusal to address himself to the critical internal problems harrassing our society; he still refused to take a position on the tough, gutty questions of our times. I was disturbed by the attitude of the actor who was playing the role of California's governor. I was disturbed by the California State Superintendent of Schools, Max Rafferty, who found answers to every ques-

tion in education by urging more law and order and who seemed
eager for a return to the McGuffy Readers. And I was disturbed
by the defeat of my friend, Senator Wayne Morse, in neighboring Oregon, and by the resignation of a close friend, Doc Howe,
as United States Commissioner of Education.

But I could also feel positive and hopeful about some things.
I had been moving around the fifty states reporting on the successful program of integration in my city of Berkeley, California.
I had spanned the country several times in thirty days and my
message was always the same: "If Berkeley did it, you can do it."
I explained that most objections to school integration were based
on myths.

No, it was not true that the Negro people were violent. Yes,
individual Negroes were violent—I could understand, but did
not condone their violence—but the violent people in our society were not the blacks. No, it was not true that Caucasian
achievement would suffer if we integrated our schools; but it was
true that minority achievement would improve if the setting for
this education could be merged with socioeconomic groups of
middle-class Americans. No, it was not true that the neighborhood school was sacrosanct; rather, it was outmoded and needed
to be replaced by an "all American model" that was educationally and economically attuned to the twentieth century. No, it
was not true that a city would become black if the powers that
be moved toward a system that would provide equal educational
opportunities for all. No, I was not discouraged over the militancy of the young students. I was pleased with their desire to
change the structure for which they had lost respect and to
restructure a system that can be relevant to them and consistent
with the times. No, I did not condone all their rebellious and,
at times, hoodlum-like techniques, but I did understand their
obvious impatience with the system. My message to them was
always the same—"Be builders, not wreckers. And while it is
fitting and proper for you to criticize, it is also your responsibility

to make constructive suggestions, and my responsibility to see that your suggestions are implemented now."

While these thoughts occurred to me often during the hearing, I was not given any leisure time to think about things in general, because counsel for the defense had one goal in mind —to discredit me as an educator qualified to react on school integration. He pounded away, hour after hour, in pursuit of this goal. He pointed out that I had spent most of my life in small, out-of-the-way school systems where the experience was not of the type that would make me knowledgeable and sensitive about problems of minority people and problems in the inner city.

He took me back to 1936 and had me report that my first teaching position was in a one-room school in the mountains of northern New Hampshire, where the student population consisted of forty-eight youngsters from grades one through eight. He did not attempt to draw from me why I started there or why I so strongly supported school integration. That job in the one-room school was the only one I, an Irish Catholic, could find at that time. I still get angry when I recall how often I was told to look for work elsewhere because there was not a Catholic church handy. I was angry then about a society that permitted employment to be affected by one's religion, so it is natural for me to be up tight now with a society that refuses to permit a man to teach because he is black or brown, or to buy a house because he is Mexican-American, or to sit at a lunch counter because of his color.

I also called to the attention of the court that this experience with forty-eight students was the beginning of my understanding of the problems of poor children being schooled under most difficult conditions. Actually, this first year of teaching was more than that—it was an exciting, rewarding experience that gave me new insights into how all children learned. I learned that Miriam, an eighth grade girl who was terminating her education and soon to be married, did a much better job working with the first grade boys than did their teacher. I learned that Billie and Ruth, in the third grade, needed to work with the fifth graders in arithmetic in order to be challenged. I learned that the best approach to science was to take all forty-eight students out of the one-room school and across the road into an open pasture where we found living evidence of what the sterile textbook was futilely calling to our attention. I found that the secret to successfully motivating the students was to love them—all of them: those who smelled of the fresh manure that they had shoveled out earlier that day; those who had body odors because they wore the same underclothing week after week; the sweet-smelling child whose mother owned the village store. Yes, I learned to love each of them and they loved me, despite my Irish-Catholic mannerisms, to which they adjusted. It was a happy, beautiful affair that lasted one year and ended with graduation in the small village hall with the youngsters showering me with tangible and intangible evidence of their love. Priscilla brought me a four-day-old lamb, which baaed during the ceremonies; Glenna brought me a necktie she had made; the parents brought me a wrist watch (my first), which caused me great concern because I knew many of them had given up something they needed in order to reward me in this way. And there were intangible things: the unspoken word, the tears (theirs and mine) that were held back, the things that only people who have come to love one another can understand.

But Counsel moved on.

"Where was your next assignment, Dr. Sullivan?"
"In Raymond, New Hampshire."
"How many students, Dr. Sullivan?"
"As I recall, about forty."
"How many grades, Dr. Sullivan?"
"Two."

It was another experience with children, in a small town in southern New Hampshire—during the middle of the depression. These children, like the children in Glencliff, were from economically deprived families, and they also responded to love and kindness and accepted me as their teacher. Here I learned that the children responded best when their parents were involved; so involve them I did. Parents made the uniforms for our baseball and basketball teams, played the old organ during our music period, and helped us develop our own school newspaper.

"And what was your next assignment, Dr. Sullivan?"

"In Derry, New Hampshire."

"And how many children, Dr. Sullivan?"

"I taught math and science to about one hundred students at the junior high level."

Here, again, was a poverty-stricken town in a small community near the Massachusetts border. The learning went on—fifty students in an eighth grade math class, with fifty different capacities to learn. I learned to individualize instruction: to Hank, who went on to the Massachusetts Institute of Technology, I taught algebra; I had to work with simple addition with Tom because he had brain damage at birth and things were not coming easily. I learned to be patient with Tom, and to push Hank with vigor.

"And then where, Dr. Sullivan?"

"To a small high school near the Vermont border in western New Hampshire."

"And how large a high school, Dr. Sullivan?"

"About two hundred fifty, I believe."

It was now 1941. I had gone to summer school every year, earned a B.S. degree, had just received my M.A. from Columbia, had married, and was terribly uneasy about conditions all around me. I watched Hitler's war machine run across Europe, was given a draft number, and tried to teach young men who also had

draft numbers. It was a most difficult year, and it got worse—
Pearl Harbor. Several of the young men left school, and before
the year was over, one of our men was killed in Bataan. More,
many more, followed.

"And then where, Dr. Sullivan?"
"To Biddeford, Maine, a textile city on the Saco River."
"How large a school, Dr. Sullivan?"
"Around three hundred, I think."
It was now 1942, and it was obvious to me that school, for the
time being, was meaningless. I went to Boston and volunteered
in the Navy, and for the next three years forgot about the intrica-
cies of making the curriculum relevant. I concentrated on survival at sea, on a destroyer in the Pacific. I was one of the
fortunate ones.

"And after the war, Dr. Sullivan?"
"I went to a small high school in central Maine—Livermore
Falls."
"How large a school, Dr. Sullivan?"
"Around two hundred fifty."
Now I met large numbers of French-Canadian children with
a language barrier—children whose parents kept them in school
until they were legally able to put them to work at the paper
mill.

"And then where, Dr. Sullivan?"
"To the neighboring community of Jay, Maine, where I be-
came the high school principal."
"And how large a school, Dr. Sullivan?"
"About two hundred students."
This was my first administrative assignment, a small high
school with a preponderance of French Canadians. The dropout
rate was in the neighborhood of 75 percent. This I had to change,

but how? Once the problem was analyzed, everything fell into place. The dropout rate was 75 percent because the local mill hired the young men at fifteen and put them on a pulp pile where most of them were to remain for the rest of their lives. The solution became obvious—approach industry; call our problem to their attention; point out that we had no vocational courses, and ask industry to take on this responsibility; use their machines and use their skilled employees as teachers; provide incentives for the youngsters by making college scholarships available to those who showed interest and ability; and, oh yes, ask industry to employ high school graduates only. This was done. We reversed the dropout rate, and a working partnership developed between industry and education.

"And then where to, Dr. Sullivan?"
"To Sanford, Maine, as Superintendent of Schools."
"How large a system, Dr. Sullivan?"
"Twenty-five hundred."

Yes, twenty-five hundred students, who in 1953 found their parents practically all unemployed. Soft goods workers, predominantly French Canadians, found themselves unemployed when the central industry, Goodall-Sanford, was purchased and then closed by Burlington Industries. What does a superintendent do under these conditions? He asks that question of the community, and the people decide. In this case, they decided they would stay and try to rebuild the town. To rebuild, they had to attrack other industries—they had to have something saleable: their skills and good schools. The decision was made to raise the taxes, build a vocational school, keep it open twenty-four hours a day, and retrain the adults from soft goods to hard goods employees. They coined the phrase "Sanford, the town that refused to die." There were twenty-four new industries in twenty-four months. The people, through their schools, had turned a successful page in community-school involvement.

"And where to next, Dr. Sullivan?"

"To East Williston, Long Island."

"How large a system, Dr. Sullivan?"

"Twenty-five hundred."

Now I was to be given a new opportunity in education. This community, containing the rich estate area of Old Westbury, home of the Vanderbilts, and Roslyn Heights, a middle-class Jewish community, had one driving desire: to develop a school system where every child would succeed. And success to these people was the entrance into and completion of work at an Ivy League school. All the ingredients necessary for success existed in this school district.

The first and most important ingredient was the right attitude, an attitude based on positivism: all children can achieve—expect nothing less from any of them. Second, they were willing to pay the price for the program. This meant recruiting on a national basis, small classes, and rich materials. Third, they were willing to have my staff introduce innovative methods. Now I tapped what I had learned in Glencliff (the nongraded school was introduced), in Raymond and Derry (individualized instruction), and in Jay and Sanford (involving the total community). Through desire, through participation, and through wise introduction of innovative techniques, a system of education was devised in which all students succeeded.

"And then where, Dr. Sullivan?"

"Prince Edward County, Virginia."

"And why Prince Edward County, Dr. Sullivan?"

Why did I go there? After all, I was comfortably located on New York's Long Island and things were going well. The system had developed a reputation for being successfully innovative. Frank Keppel, the then incumbent United States Commissioner of Education, had just visited the schools and had enthusiastically supported the programs being carried on in the schools. I had just been given another four-year contract with a substantial pay increase.

But I was not happy. The challenge no longer existed for me in a tranquil suburban community. The challenge was obviously in the city, but why be concerned? And why go to Prince Edward County? Because the man who was assassinated on June 5, 1968, in the city of Los Angeles, asked me to go there. His brother, President John F. Kennedy, could no longer tolerate the behavior of the officials of Prince Edward County, who had closed their public schools rather than comply with the Supreme Court decision in *Brown* v. *Board of Education.* They had opened private schools for the white children.

In Prince Edward County I discovered the most beautiful people anywhere in the world. I found children so anxious to learn that they would go to school seven days a week, twelve months a year. They refused to go home when the water supply was exhausted. They asked the staff to come to school during the days set aside for state conferences. Yes, these were beautiful, patient people who still believed that equal opportunities would be theirs someday soon, even though they saw the white power structure in Virginia defy the Supreme Court of the United States. But that September in 1963 they had hope because Attorney General Robert Kennedy was reopening schools. I was privileged to be selected as the person to do the reopening. It was a wonderful year for me because it was a stimulating, rewarding year for the children.

The project was a massive dose of compensatory education, richly supported by groups such as the Ford Foundation and helped by people who could (like the little girl in St. Paul, Minnesota, who contributed 347 pennies from her piggie bank). The program proved what I knew all the time—any group of children can achieve if you have sufficient money and the right people working with the children. It proved something else, though. Children educated in complete isolation will indeed achieve under proper conditions, but their attitudes toward other races will harden.

"And then where, Dr. Sullivan?"

"Berkeley, California."

"How many students, Dr. Sullivan?"

"Sixteen thousand."

"By the way, Dr. Sullivan, how many square miles in the City of Berkeley?"

"About twenty."

I had been happy to join the community of Berkeley, a community wanting to do something about all this—and doing it. Berkeley believed that the best way—the only way—to change attitudes and to improve achievement was through quality integrated schools. The Berkeley school system did what was morally, legally, and educationally right. They stated categorically that you could not have quality education without integration. The city doubled its tax rate in order to build a system of *equality* education, and became the first city in the United States with a population over one hundred thousand (with a large black population—42 percent in the schools) to completely integrate grades kindergarten through twelve. Berkeley was the first city to introduce two-way busing, thus keeping the schools in the black ghetto open and moving white children into them. The community also believed that the best way to encourage minorities to enter the teaching profession was to state publicly that the district was going to employ large numbers of qualified minorities at every level within the educational system.

Berkeley is also a city that has more black militants, proportionately, than most cities in America. In this case, the black militants supported integration. The city has a high percentage of elite, sophisticated Caucasians who said "Yes, integrate, but give our children something at the end of the bus ride." And there were those who resisted. The local newspaper fought school integration. The city has a high percentage of "Birchers" who also fought change every step of the way.

While it is true that Berkeley is smaller by far than Los Angeles, it is not true that it is or was easier to integrate. We had all the dimensions to work with—some more complicated than Los Angeles. And Berkeley succeeded. If Berkeley can do it, any city can and should do it. The success Berkeley is enjoying can be enjoyed by Los Angeles, if the leaders stop vacillating, stop procrastinating, and do what is legal and right.

The cross examination came to a grinding stop, but the last words had not been uttered. The counsel for the plaintiff asked me a few questions.

"Dr. Sullivan, have you worked in any other cities as a consultant?"

"Yes, Portland, Oregon; Seattle, Washington; Oklahoma City, Oklahoma; Galveston, Texas; Denver, Colorado; Phoenix, Arizona; Buffalo, New York; to name a few."

"Dr. Sullivan, tell the court where your next assignment is."

"I am going to Massachusetts on January 1 to become Commissioner of Education there."

"How many students will be under your supervision?"

"Around one million five hundred thousand."

Finally the judge asked the last question of the counsel for the defense.

"And Mr. Berman, how many students would you say were in Los Angeles?"

18

The Role of the Educator

Dedication to People

Before the action starts in a football game, the team and the coaches or umpires or managers meet to review the rules of the game and to plan the action. Then each player, when he gets into the game, gives his all—but never loses sight of the whole team! He fully understands the ground rules. Before any team embarks on a project, whether that team is made up of lay citizens, students, fellow administrators, teachers, or any other group, the members must go over the rules step by step, again and again, until the rules are perfectly clear and interpreted in the same way by everyone. If some of the rules get in the way or create semantic problems, clear up the differences in interpretation and understanding *before* launching the project. Then, full steam ahead!

This is what I have tried to do during my years as an administrator. I have regarded my staff as my team and have called them together frequently and regularly to discuss the rules and action of the game. We have met both individually and collectively to advise, consider, suggest, criticize constructively, or praise the ideas or actions of the team and its members. Then I have left the field to them, giving each member full responsibility for his position on the team, and expecting each one to carry his responsibility. Either I have sufficient confidence in him to give him full power in his field or we cannot work together.

A perfect example of a meritorious project that failed initially is the Oceanside-Brownsville project in Brooklyn, New York City's first attempt at community control. There were extremely talented men in this project: the district principal, the superintendent of schools, the president of the New York Federation of Teachers, and the Commissioner of Education in New York. The project, a bold departure and a worthwhile attempt at decentralization, also received help from the Ford Foundation. Tragically, the project resulted in a major teachers' strike in our largest city. Why? Because the ground rules had not been established clearly enough for the participating parties to interpret them in the same way.

Teachers and students are no longer willing to sit by passively and let administrators think and decide for them. This is the way the game used to be played, and, generally, the students and the teachers came out losers. The administrators' accomplishments, if there were any, were not always those desired by the students or the staff. Students, teachers, and staff all prefer to participate in the action, and even to have some of it all to themselves. And why not? Isn't that what education is all about—to prepare people to take their unique and individual places in the world? (That is why I want the young people and the teachers of Massachusetts to advise me on conditions and needs in our schools. I want them not only to inform and advise me, but also to make their recommendations to the state board of education—to tell the board what they tell me.)

A school administrator must be able to communicate. He must care about people in general—old people, black people, middle-aged people, women people, men people, white people, you-name-it people—he must care about them all. It is amazing how readily attitudes, however artfully concealed, can be communicated. Don't think for a minute if you have a hangup about black people that you can hide it! Don't think for a minute if you are uncomfortable about having little old ladies around you that you can hide these feelings from them. Don't get the idea that a physically handicapped person does not know immediately if you are uneasy in his presence! You are not hard to read. It is not easy to rid our minds and feelings of these deep-seated, perhaps even unconscious, prejudices, but we had better do just that if we are to remain in education.

The best way to open our minds is to open our hearts and seek out people who have never before been part of our circle. Talk with them, work with them, visit with them, play with them, listen to them—this is how we get to know them, and they get to know us. From this may not come perfect agreement, but there does come mutual trust and respect. We must do this with the community, with the leaders and the "little people," with the staff, and with the students. We must share with them the responsibility of exchanging information and ideas to better the schools.

I strongly urge every school administrator to visit city hall and the corridors and offices of the state legislature to see our civic leaders, our legislative leaders, and their aides at work. Move about into the urban-suburban areas, meet group leaders (especially the leaders of all the minority groups), have a go with the labor-management groups, and become personally immersed in some of the critical problems in our cities and towns.

Many of my colleagues feel that a school superintendent should take an X number of methods courses—and an X number of hours in the history of education—and several courses in educational philosophy—and, oh yes, make sure he has taken courses in psychology, school management, school law, curriculum development, and at least a dozen other similar subjects. I could go on enumerating course requirements that the various states insist upon for an administrative credential. The list is a long one. On the other hand, there seems to be a trend toward the belief that because of the growing complexity of the school superintendent's job, he need not necessarily be an expert in education. Perhaps it would be better for him to have a big-business background, since he has such vast amounts of money to handle, such a large staff, and so many housing, maintenance, and merchandising problems. In larger school districts the superintendent has a team of specialists to whom he can turn over the specialized areas of concern: a business manager, a maintenance coordinator, a personnel director, an assistant superintendent for curriculum, various directors and coordinators of public relations, special education, elementary and secondary curriculum, libraries, and so forth.

I agree that certification procedures for school administrators are necessary. The one pitch I would make would be that a man's background be rich in the humanities. I would put the onus on schools of higher education to focus on uniform, minimum standards. (I point with pride to the pioneering work done in this area by schools such as Harvard, Wisconsin, and Stanford.) And I agree that the superintendent's job is becoming even more complex, and that the business aspects are among the superintendent's major responsibilities. I also welcome the development of the supervisory team, that group of experts who share in the administration of the larger school districts.

But the foremost quality needed to be a successful, effective school administrator is the ability to empathize and to communicate with young people. The superintendent must never lose sight of or contact with the most important group of all, the students themselves. When I selected this profession over thirty years ago, I did so because I was interested in youth. That interest has intensified in the course of my career and is as strong today as Commissioner of Education as it was when I was a superintendent of schools, and, years before that, when I was a teacher. If I am to be effective, it is essential that I relate to the students in our schools, not only to establish rapport, but also to keep my own incentive—as well as theirs—alive and stimulated. Unless the administrator has worked directly with students in classroom situations, he cannot be fully aware of either the learning problems of the students or the classroom problems of the teacher. To understand fully the job of each member of the supervisory team, the administrator must know how it affects the children who are being educated and the teachers who are in direct contact with the children. Every educator, however high he is in the administrative echelon, should go back into the classroom periodically to keep his hand in that part of the action.

I have done this as often as I could all through my years as an administrator. These direct contacts with the children, the teachers, and the classroom have been among my happiest times. In addition to giving me pleasure, however, these contacts have given the children an opportunity to meet and see in action the man who makes the wheels go round. The experiences have also kept me sensitized to the children, the teachers, the curriculum, and the classroom situation. I recommend this practice to all school administrators for their pleasure and their own continuing education.

I have found public school work to be a challenging and rewarding profession. I recommend it highly. Can you relate to people? Do you enjoy, appreciate, understand, and respect young people? Do you care about *all* people? If so, you are urgently needed in our profession.